MARTIN EVE REMEMBERED

Dedicated to all the team of consultants, medical specialists, doctors, nurses, Marie Curie nurses, physiotherapists and occupational therapists who cared for Martin and made the last twelve years possible, especially:

Dr Norman Parker	Consultant Haematologist
Dr John Scadding	Consultant Neurologist
Dr Fiona C. Moore	Consultant in Rehabilitation
Dr Nicholas Dodd	Consultant Haematologist
Mr. Terry Mott	Consultant Oncologist
Mr Simon Huddy	Consultant Surgeon
Wendy Carragher	Oncology Nurse
Jean Cass	Hospice Nurse

Martin Eve Remembered

Edited by Walter Kemsley

Merlin Press
1999

First published in 1999
By the Merlin Press Ltd
2 Rendlesham Mews, Rendlesham
Nr. Woodbridge, Suffolk
IP12 2SZ

© The Merlin Press 1999

ISBN   085036 485 X

Cover by Louis Mackay from original charcoal
drawing by Walter Kemsley

Privateer on inside-back cover from original
photograph by Den Phillips

Typesetting by Julie Rainford

Printed in Finland by WSOY

ACKNOWLEDGEMENTS

Grateful thanks to all those who have contributed
to the writing and production of this story.

INTRODUCTION

When Martin Eve died in 1998 publishing lost a remarkable free spirit and the socialist-humanist cause a staunch advocate, who helped that cause by publishing the works of talented authors of different nationalities from such unlikely offices as a derelict warehouse and a former builder's yard in what was then unfashionable Docklands.

Martin Weston Eve was born in 1924 after his parents had settled at Orford on the Suffolk coast, and Orford was his home during boyhood and early manhood. His father, T.L.B. Eve, a well-known yachtsman, came of Maldon merchant stock. Martin's music-loving mother, who was partly of Huguenot descent, was a daughter of Dr. William Orange, C.B., the first deputy superintendent and second superintendent of Broadmoor Criminal Lunatic Asylum. She was a Fabian Socialist, and after marriage was an active rural district councillor, following her pre-marriage career as a sanitary inspector and housing officer. Martin's life showed his heritage from both his parents. Already a talented pianist and organist, he was to become, as Merlin Press, a publisher who sought to further Socialist aims for the betterment of mankind, and he brought to the readership of his Seafarer Books imprint a love of sailing and the sea, which developed from very early instruction by his father on the Ore and the Alde. His entry into publishing followed schooldays as a chorister at Winchester Cathedral and scholar at Bryanston, wartime service in the Royal Navy, and a Cambridge history degree. He founded Merlin Press in 1956 and added Seafarer Books in 1968. With a very small staff, and doing, as was necessary, everything himself - from reading manuscripts to packing and delivering books by motorbike and even abroad by his old smack-yacht - he kept going as an independent publisher with a cause when publishing became increasingly absorbed by 'big business'. And he managed this in later years in spite of crippling illness. His helpfulness, sincerity, good humour and understanding brought him a wide circle of friends in publishing, politics and sailing, and he won their admiration by his twelve-year fight against disease, which ended with his death in his native Suffolk in October, 1998.

This book is a collection of tributes to Martin written by family, friends, colleagues, comrades, and authors to celebrate a rich and varied life. The tributes have been assembled to follow the course of that life from its early years.

The book also includes his own account of the early years of Merlin Press: the completed part of a history begun in his last year after he had taken his work from London to the land of his roots.

Walter Kemsley
Brother-in-law

CONTENTS

Early Days Pilgrims' School Anthony Caesar
Bryanston Dr C.W.L. Smith
Wartime Edward Fawcett
Karel Citroen

Cambridge Days Dr Julian Tudor Hart
Dorothy Thompson

Family Recollections Mary Kemsley
Christopher Eve
Catherine Eve
William Eve
Laurie Eve

Merlin Press: Early Years Martin Eve
Ian Kiek
Ian Norrie

Socialist Register Marion Kozak
Leo Panitch

Life at Merlin Press Louis Mackay
Bill Norris
Tina Craig
Sarah Tisdall
Munro Moore
Aghdas Bidhendi
Natalie Jones

Merlin Authors Gordon Leff
István Mészáros
Sheila Rowbotham
Francis Beckett
Adrian Hogben

Seafarer Authors Anthony Bailey
Henry Swain
Rayner Unwin

CONTENTS (CONT'D)

Seafaring Days		John Wainwright
		Gill Jacobs
		John Maxwell
Friends		Dr Michael Hathorn
		Mary Hoseason
		John Mahon
Drawing The Threads Together		Walter Kemsley
		Dr John Scadding
Obituaries	*Guardian*	John Saville
	Independent	David Musson
	Bookseller	David Musson
	East Anglian	Richard Smith
	Gaffers Log	George Jago
	Old Gaffers Association	
Poetry Farewell		Walter Kemsley

EARLY DAYS

A FIFTY-YEAR GAP

Just before Christmas 1933 *The Times* newspaper published a splendid photograph of Winchester Cathedral choir in processional order in the beautiful retrochoir, supposedly on their way to sing the annual carol service.

In front of the sixteen choristers in their white surplices and ruffs, together with the six lay-clerks, the Precentor and the Sacrist, there were three young boys in purple gowns and Eton collars and facing them all was Dr Harold Rhodes, the organist and master of the choristers.

The three purple-clad boys were the Probationers hoping to qualify before too long as full choristers. The tallest was called Ollerenshaw, next to him was Caesar, and behind them was Eve - surnames only was the custom in those pre-war prep school days!

I had arrived at The Pilgrims' School, the Cathedral Choir School, for the summer term 1933 aged just nine and Martin followed in September. We must have struck up a good friendship during the following five years because I remember his kind and (so they seemed) elderly parents taking me out to lunch at the Guest House just below Westgate, where they were staying, on more than one occasion. And once, during a school holiday, probably in August 1937, I stayed at their home, Rosehill, in Orford and went sailing in their dinghy along the river Alde.

There were various highlights during those years, including an outing by boat to see the Silver Jubilee Naval review in the Solent in 1935; a choir singing-tour in Jersey and Guernsey, the Channel Islands belonging to the Diocese of Winchester; the Deanery Turkey Feast in the winter and the Strawberry Feast in the summer; the attendance at a service by the Duke and Duchess of York shortly before they became King George VI and Queen Elizabeth.

Most of the time, of course, we were hard at it in class-room, on playing field and in daily choir practices for the nine or ten services we sang every week for a good forty-two weeks each year, including staying at school over Christmas which was actually great fun.

I honestly cannot remember how good Martin was at work, or games, or music, but anyone who survived five years at The Pilgrims' in those days can't have been bad at any of them! I believe he made a few close friendships rather than a wider circle of acquaintances. In 1938 I departed for Cranleigh School and Martin for Bryanston and we soon lost touch.

Fifty years later, when I was working in London as Sub-Dean of H.M. Chapels Royal, Martin got in touch quite out of the blue and invited me to supper with Pat in their home in Savernake Road, NW3. It was wonderful to renew friendship after such a gap and to meet Pat for the first time.

Another ten years passed and then, as I began a holiday in East Anglia last August, I made it my first port of call to visit Martin and Pat in their home near Woodbridge. He and I enjoyed a good talk about many things of common interest and concern, alas for the last time, for he died eleven weeks later.

For me, Martin was a deeply thoughtful and caring person and I am grateful for having known him, however fitfully, for those sixty-five years.

Anthony Caesar
School friend

* * *

MEMOIRS OF MARTIN EVE   DR C.W.L. SMITH

I shared quite a lot with Martin. We started at Bryanston School together, in September 1936. We found the ledge round the huge centre room lined with tins of condensed milk, which to our surprise turned out to be for Republican Spain.

Over those wooden dining tables, I learnt where Orford Ness was. In a storm a sailing boat had been lost off the Ness and Martin, who lived at Orford, filled in the newspaper descriptions; and it remained in my imagination.

I recall his writing a nice piece for the school magazine on the joys of playing the harmonium. I, who was editor, edited it unwisely; I think his complaint about this jumped-up editorial power was a formative influence on both of us.

There were other shared topics: the good and heroic things about the Soviet Union and the anti-fascist movement of those hectic days - pretty hectic even in the beautiful faraway grounds of Bryanston; as, for instance, the fighting with the Hitler Youth among the Salem school exchange of 1938.

For many years I saw nothing of Martin, until, in the 70s, after the painful end of his first marriage, I began seeing him in a new role, as his G.P. Soon I met Will, and then Pat, and much later Cathy and Chris.

We compared our mutual experiences in Yugoslavia in 1947-48, especially the songs of the railway and road builders, which Martin sang at the piano, much better than I.

We, my wife and I, were intrigued by his careful single-handed publishing and how he offered Sarah Tisdall, in prison for breaking the Official Secrets Act in the early 80s, a job for her release, which she kept for 2 years.

Then began that advancing neuropathy related to lymphoma and a fractured hip, which put him on to crutches; on and on, relentlessly and pitilessly, through 12 years. He was fortunate enough to be given a place for intensive re-habilitation at St Joseph's. But from his stay there, he took away an empathy with such disablement and such resources of self-help as I had not met before - the sticks, the crutches, the gadgets and tricks; but most of all the care of Pat.

After my retirement and their move to Rendlesham, Viking country, and Merlin's move to Rendlesham, Martin suffered a carcinoma of the colon and liver.

Last spring he was involved with the 150th anniversary of the Communist Manifesto, in line with his continued serious thinking about that long and noble tradition, like his 30 years of publishing *Socialist Register*.

They sailed their boat *Privateer* up to a year or two ago. Pat undertook body training so she could lift the anchor and man this or that for her ailing husband. Then, after selling the beloved boat to a fitting owner, they had a party at Pin Mill last June, for Seafarer Books; for the sailors and writers and boat-builders and printers; where Martin sat, grey and tired, but attentive, often funny, and very alive. It was a celebration, of the life afloat, the making of books and boats: Merlin was publishing up to the end; but now they had no boat - it was also a farewell.

And with love to Pat.

Bill Smith
School friend, lifelong friend and G.P.

* * *

LIFE ON *TALYBONT*   EDWARD FAWCETT

"There's the new Mid. Come and have a look". We were standing by the building of the Hunt class destroyer *Talybont* at Sammy White's yard at Cowes and there indeed was Martin walking gloomily down the other side of the street.

Somewhat unusually for an R.N.V.R. officer, Martin was an excellent seaman. He had been brought up in boats, as became clear when we sailed the ship's dinghy at Scapa Flow. His family home was at Orford and his father, austere and ascetic, taught him all that a small-boat sailor needed to know.

Martin and I became friends while walking round Rame Head when *Talybont* was based on Devonport. His political opinions were always more advanced than mine, but we could discuss anything and were never angry. We also took various Wren friends sailing on the Hamoaze and went to *The Girl of the Golden West* at the Theatre Royal. Happy days.

Martin was an excellent organist, so whenever we came to a church on our walks in we went (not locked in those days) and I was treated to a recital or worked the bellows.

Martin's action station was in charge of the plot in the wheelhouse, so he was an important figure in the disastrous battle off Les Sept Isles, Brittany, when four Elbing destroyers sank the anti-aircraft cruiser Charybdis and the Ledbury, leader of the destroyer screen. Our 'headache' radio received all the plain-language messages from the Elbings as they discharged their torpedoes, which our Dutch radio-operator, Karel Citroen translated. This information was apparently not available to Charybdis who continued her course unaltered, to be hit ten minutes later by four torpedoes. The Elbings, and the merchant ship they were escorting, returned triumphantly to harbour. All this was recorded on Martin's plot.

Our 'D' Day orders were not promising. We were to bombard a battery of heavy guns, protected by massive concrete turrets, on the top of the Point du Hoc, which commanded Omaha Beach. At 4000 yards they could not have missed and neither Martin nor I expected to return. The guns turned out to be dummies!

Although I think we sank a German trawler in a night battle, we definitely sank a British one, the Florence Desmond, in a midnight collision off Lundy Island. Martin and Tony Griffin had just taken over the Middle Watch from myself and Johnny Beaumont. We reported having seen a light ahead which subsequently disappeared. We were escorting the battleship, King George V, and were not allowed to use radar, so couldn't verify what it was. Ten minutes later it felt as if we had hit a mine; we had passed several on the surface during the afternoon. Actually it was Florence Desmond. We had wrecked our bows, but she was sinking. Nobody was hurt.

The damage was sufficient for *Talybont* to de-commission. Martin and I went our different ways. Friendship continued and included happy family skiing holidays, enlivened by an intake of Steinhager, an electrifying Schnapps.

Talk about everything and everybody was what brought us together; we were light hearted and we laughed a lot. It was a very happy friendship.

These verses, I hope, capture the spirit of that happy friendship.

Aground

Do you feel we're going slower?
Not that we were going fast!
Should the bow-wave not be higher?
Shame that good puff didn't last.

Nothing nasty here to scare us,
Open sea for miles around.
Seeming stillness just a fuss,
No, we cannot be aground!

Perish such ignoble thinking,
For we have a perfect fix,
From that starboard buoy a bobbing,
Lighthouse bearing Oh One Six!

May I have the glasses Martin?
Did you say the buoy was red?
How did you describe the top-mark?
Is that really what you said?

Alas, perhaps we were mistaken.
Such a buoy does not exist!
Perhaps the right-hand lens was broken;
Must have been a touch of mist.

Stuck we are there is no question,
Stuck upon a falling tide.
We shall not be back for luncheon,
Tea is botched, and much beside.

Back at home our wives, unknowing,
Chat and pass the time away,
But we know what they'll be saying
Later on this fateful day.

"We should never have allowed it,
They have no idea of time,
Bet they're stuck upon the Wallet -"
Yes, Stuck upon the Wallet ... Yet again!

Teddy Fawcett
Fellow Naval Officer

* * *

MARTIN, *TALYBONT* AND ME

KAREL CITROEN

When fresh from a torpedoing and subsequent 'Survivors' Leave,' I joined *HMS Talybont* in November 1943 and representing a one-man department in her, I was told to mess and to bunk with the Officers' stewards.

Very soon Martin sensed that I was not quite happy there. With his inborn tact he did not tell me this, but he proposed that I share his cabin - in which there was hardly space for one. That was the beginning of a beautiful friendship.

Martin did more: to a war orphan, away from his occupied country, he gave moral support. Again, he never indicated this with so much as one word, but he started talking about his Bryanston days and his political beliefs, topics he could not share with any of his brother-officers; but in me he found a ready listener.

We shared another activity: he asked me to assist him with the ship's administration and correspondence, the latter including many pieces of remarkable nonsense emanating from The Secretary of the Admiralty. For these Martin created a special file, apart from the sixteen regular ones in which the ship's papers were stowed; this 'File Seventeen' consisted of the port-hole.

We also shared censoring ratings' outgoing letters and found to our amused amazement that for certain frequently recurring words the sailors used variations unknown to two lettered public schoolboys.

With many of his fellow-countrymen Martin shared that very British characteristic: a stiff upper lip, with this difference that his was not a rigid, but a supple one. He reminded and still reminds me of the legend on a Victorian easy chair with arm-rests formed as dogs: 'Gentle when stroked, fierce when provoked.'

Goodbye, Martin, steadiest of shipmates, finest of friends.

Karel Citroen
Comrade at sea

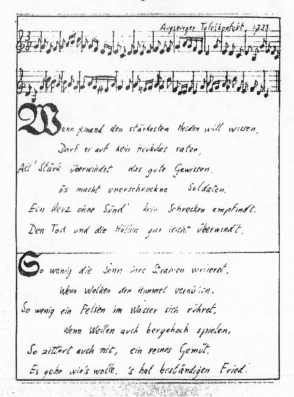

A translation of the requiem follows:

When trying to search for the strongest of heroes
We must never come upon Hercules' name.
All craft is defeated by the good conscience,
Which bodies forth warriors and men of fame.
A heart without vice no fear undergoes,
Death, hell it will conquer, as well as its foes.

So little the sun its rays shall be losing
When clouds are concealing the heavens above.
So little a rock in the sea shall be shaking
When waves are gushing as high as a hill,
So do never tremble, because a pure soul
Is constantly peaceful, may come what will.

Composed by Karel Citroen

* * *

CAMBRIDGE DAYS

A PEACE HERO   DR JULIAN TUDOR HART

I first met Martin in 1947. We were students at adjacent colleges at Cambridge, and were both members of the University Communist Party students' branch. Like Martin, about 80% of the male students were ex-servicemen, and some of our branch members had witnessed the British intervention against ELAS and the Greek Communists at first hand. There was a general feeling among us that though winning the peace might be more difficult than winning the war, it would be infinitely less dangerous and uncomfortable. So we should work hard and not complain.

My first impressions of Martin never changed. Apart from a little superficial exterior ageing, nor did he. He had great personal charm, and seemed to have been born wise. He began and ended as a seriously committed democratic socialist of a steady and sustainable sort, concerned to be useful, his expectations adapted to a continually receding horizon. He seemed much better prepared than most of us to pursue this visible but always remote objective, without worrying too much about the troubles he met on the way. In 1948 the Party contorted itself into one of its more absurd Yoga positions, echoing every syllable of Stalin's denunciation of Tito, backed by a book by James Klugman (who had served in Yugoslavia as a British liaison officer with the partisans). Internationally, Communists organised themselves into yet another International, not the 4th because that might entail confusion with the Tr*tsky*tes, nor the 5th because that would accept that Tr*tsky*sm had actually existed, just the Communist Information Bureau or COMINFORM. This published a newspaper, advertised by a poster of a boy in a cloth cap with a bundle of papers under one arm, his hand cupped to augment his cry to workers to buy *For a Lasting Peace and a People's Democracy!* We renamed it *For For*. So far as I know no real worker ever bought it, and certainly nobody read it for any reason other than to marvel at its many pages of dense print, unrelieved by pictures, which seemed to be leaden translations of wooden editorials from *Pravda*.

Why on earth did we do it? Because for most of us at the time, and a few of us ever since, this seemed almost completely irrelevant to something else far more important and enduring, which was simply not to be had in the Labour Party. Marxist ideas, from people who actually read what the two old beards wrote and undertook practical activities in the labour movement in which to test theory with practice, had produced a generation of intellectual giants. These included many manual workers with little formal education, as well as outstanding figures in science and the arts who profoundly influenced progressive opinion from about 1935 to 1948, far beyond the Party's membership. Few of these had found any welcome in the Labour Party. The clearest voices on the Labour left depended on Communists to initiate the few active campaigns they ever persuaded the Labour Party to endorse. The Party had a powerful educational workforce and organisation, providing a firm grounding in simple socialist ideas. Such education virtually disappeared from the Labour Party after the first world war. Some of this was rubbish, but it was not too hard to separate this from the gold.

All the Cambridge Communists endlessly discussed these ideas, and also the many ways in which they were denied by what we could see of command socialism in practice. Martin spent the rest of his life developing them, eventually without the heavy excess baggage entailed in Communist Party membership, particularly as it lost its trade union base. He published serious contributors to a British radical tradition stretching back to the English Civil War, and forward well into the future: Martin had a good eye for what would last, and unlike most modern publishers, never destroyed old stock.

After about 40 years of only exchanging Christmas cards, I met Martin again in 1987, to discuss publishing *A New Kind of Doctor*. Already badly disabled by spinal cord damage from his lymphoma, he loped along the street in the Isle of Dogs to his Dickensian warehouse, talking as we went. I was barely able to keep up with him because I was much shorter, and like him, was becoming an old man. By then, Lawrence and Wishart was well on its way to post-modernism, and was preparing the ground for the Ex-Marxist Mutual Admiration Society (known variously as the Emmas or the Jaquerie), which helps Tony Blair to evolve beyond Thatcher.

Martin was a Peace Hero. We did not, after all, win the peace, but his lifetime of work helped us not altogether to lose it.

Julian Tudor Hart
Kindred spirit, Cambridge, Merlin author

* * *

LIFELONG FRIENDSHIP   DOROTHY THOMPSON

Martin has been so much a part of my and my family's life that it is difficult to know where to start.

Perhaps one point would be the remark made to me recently by a writer friend to the effect that one of the mysteries of modern letters was why Edward published with Merlin Press. Trying to answer this absurdity meant trying to explain to him that for Edward publishing was not purely a commercial matter but part of a complex project. We saw many aspects and periods of our life in this way, and looking back many of the most important projects involved Martin.

This has to be a short piece so there is not space to look at all the projects we were involved in. There was the whole episode of the establishment of a European New Left after 1956, - the *Reasoner*, *The New Reasoner* and the pamphlets and other publications involved. We all took part in CND and marched from Aldermaston, but END was more difficult and more particular and would have been impossible - or at least very different - without both Edward and Merlin. Then there were family projects - Martin and Betty and the children came to our Welsh house and most of our family, e*n masse* or in smaller groups, sailed in *Privateer* and learnt what little we know about sailing in her. Edward crewed across the channel, Ben when he lived at Thorpe-le-Soken turned out to crew on occasion, and there were adventures in which we were all at some time involved as well as week-ends too stormy to sail spent with a bottle of Scotch and a guitar safe at mooring. Nearly all Edward's later books and those which have been published since he died were published by Merlin and were partly edited and arranged by Martin.

We all met in Cambridge immediately after the war. I had done two years of my degree course before call-up, Edward had done one year and Martin was starting, having gone straight from school into the navy. We were all reading history and we were all members of the Communist Party. The CP in the University was, for us all I think, a new kind of politics. We started to look not only at political action but at Marxism as a philosophy and a theoretical system. We discovered Vico and Linguet and a variety of names not on the syllabus and organised our own seminars to discuss them. We worked out a lengthy critique of the Cambridge History syllabus the details of which I no longer remember, but I know they included a strong objection to the study of political thought as a discrete tradition quite separate from the social context of the ideas.

In the summer of 1947 a group of us signed on with a reconstruction project to help with the building of a railway in Jugoslavia. It was on the youth railway that the three of us worked together for the first time. I have just been re-reading, after a gap of many years, the small book that we produced about it in 1948. The main text is written by Edward and there is a chapter by me about the British Brigade and one by Martin on Recreation. Some of the other contributors are still friends, a few are no longer alive, but the book brings back very good memories. When we arrived in Jugoslavia the British organisation was sloppy and inefficient. A very British revolution took place in which the whole brigade - around a hundred members - held a meeting and replaced the middle-aged representatives of the British - Jugoslav Society with elected officers and a committee. Edward was elected commandant, I was secretary and Martin 'cultural officer,' though he preferred the title of 'choirmaster'. For the rest of the summer - from mid-July to September - we organised the work, the papers and the recreational activities of the various groups of Brits who passed through. There were other 'officers,' the British representative on the Railway newspaper, the foremen of the two working parties and a deputy commandant who had been ADC to General Montgomery and who smartened up the camp and the working programme. From six in the morning until about two in the afternoon we worked on the rock face with picks, shovels and wheelbarrows. Under our new regime officers worked as well as other brigade members. After a short siesta we organised evening events from informal sing-songs around a bonfire in one or another of the brigades' camps to more formal concerts and recitals. Martin struggled hard to discipline the British choir, which even the Albanians described as 'barbaric,' and did at least persuade them to sing 'The Lincolnshire Poacher' and 'The Foggy Foggy Dew' in time and in tune under his baton. I meanwhile wrestled with the papers and passports of two hundred and odd Britons all of whom appeared to want to set off in different directions through occupied post-war Europe after they left the camp. When Edward and I visited the district in 1979 we could find no trace of the Youth Railway, so it may be that the most important things we built there were the friendships, both with the Jugoslavs and with other members of our own and other foreign brigades. Many of the people we met there we met again in the years immediately after the Krushchev speech of 1956 taking part in the attempt to build a non-aligned European Left.

In England we always seemed to live at some distance from Martin and his family geographically. This meant that when we did get together it was for several days or for special events. We walked in our holiday part of Wales or sailed and ate oysters in the waters round Essex and Suffolk. We met at the Aldeburgh Festival or in London for music, plays or operas, or stayed at each other's houses. Telephone communication was frequent and entertaining and I still miss our conversations. Martin was a friend, a sympathetic critic and a publisher, and he was an essential part of our lives for half a century.

Dorothy Thompson
Fellow Student Cambridge, Lifelong friend

* * *

BUILDING A DAM IN BULGARIA

In 1948 Martin was one of the party which helped to construct the Georgi
Dimitrov Dam at Koprinka in Bulgaria. Early every morning this song
was sung by the British Frank Thompson Brigade marching to work with
pick and shovel.

Oh Youth come forth in emulation
The rising hope of all our nation
Lift up your picks, your banners red,
A waving forest overhead, high overhead.
Cheer them triumphant in their labour
Rejoicing each man with his neighbour
Who build a land which none shall mar
Hurrah, hurrah, hurrah!

Behold our rivers in their swift flow
And hark our valleys as they speak low
Deep throated is our tractor's shout
And over all youth's voice cries out, youth's voice cries out.
To whom then are our forests singing,
To whom our blue hills welcome bringing?
And lakes so clear and luminous
To us, to us, to us!

Then go brigades with inspiration
To factory and irrigation
Our towns and mines await us now
So let us make a solemn vow - a solemn vow.
For homeland built on right and truth
For our invincible proud youth
For our great Georgi Dimitrov
March off, march off, march off!

* * *

FAMILY RECOLLECTIONS

SISTER'S VIEW   MARY KEMSLEY

I am very fortunate to have had Martin as my brother. He was just as good-natured and easy to get on with as a child as he was later. In the 1920s and 1930s it was safe for children to go off on their own or with friends, so we took advantage of all that Orford offered - sailing, rowing, swimming and cycling. Martin took after our father in having a great aptitude for sailing.

Martin also inherited from my mother's family perfect pitch and a great gift for music. When very young he was exceptionally good at the piano, singing, and playing the organ. He played at a christening service when his feet could only just reach the pedals. He won a music scholarship to the Pilgrims' School, Winchester, and sang in the Cathedral choir. Some years later I remarked to him that I had been sorry for him when he had to remain at Winchester during part of the Christmas and Easter holidays. He said that he loved singing in such a good choir. After the war Martin played the piano until the progressive loss of the use of his hands made all piano-playing impossible.

In wartime, although Martin was in the Navy and I was in the A.T.S., we managed to see each other sometimes. He visited me when he was an Ordinary Seaman and was the cause of a totally unscheduled 'Eyes Right' by an entire squad of A.T.S. marching by. I once went aboard *H.M.S. Talybont* at Portsmouth.

After the war we kept in touch and visited each other's families, and for the last few years of his life, he lived very near us. We were able to see how very bravely and uncomplainingly a previously very active man put up with terrible and extensive disabilities, which got slowly worse for years, and then rapidly worse as his death approached. Pat's wonderful love and care made his last years more bearable. He derived pleasure from his three children and seven grandchildren all doing well, and from his many friends.

Mary Kemsley
Sister

* * *

MARTIN'S DEATH AND BEYOND   CHRISTOPHER EVE

About forty-five years ago, as I began to talk, Martin started a conversation with me (as his own extraordinary father had with him) which continued up to his death, resuming whenever we met. He taught me, from the age of two, that thinking is fun, that there is no last word, that a cat's word is as good as a king's, that thinking is indispensable to sorting the world out, and that understanding the world and sorting it out is a sensible and natural human goal. He also taught me the enormous value and, at the same time, the routine deep inadequacy of the corpus of published knowledge. Ideas were what drove and captivated him, and he was fascinating to talk with because he usually had an original and thought-provoking view, as well as a really encyclopaedic knowledge of political events in all periods.

I never saw Martin bitter or in fear of anything or anyone, and his approach to his death was in character with this. A few weeks before he died he asked to speak to each of his family separately, and when he spoke to me thus he ensured that we both said to each other the things we needed to say, with the result that, unusually, I don't feel bad at all about his dying - only sad.

Up to the end his conversational and questing spirit flourished unchecked, and in his last weeks he spoke to me of the campaign he felt the Left needed to mount against a recrudescent Eugenics (and of his part in it as a publisher), wondered why the Basque nation, uniquely amongst Europeans, seem able to run large scale and durable cooperatives; suggested that Shaw's great gift was his ability to beguile, as Ibsen could not, the philistines who constituted London theatre audiences before the Great War.

In his last hours, Martin told his assembled, extended family that he'd had a marvellous life which he'd enjoyed enormously and now he wanted to end it. As he drifted towards coma, he still kept that familiar humorous quirk of the mouth.

Death is a hard problem for Humanists. Martin was not running out of important things to say, so I have to see his death as wasteful. I agree very much with Shaw, in the preface to *Back to Methuselah* where he says that seventy years is barely a sufficient adolescence, that it is just when people have learnt enough to be useful that they die, and that this is wrong and should be redressed. But I feel lucky to have had such a good seventy-four years out of him. The very many conversations he started, both in person and through book publishing, will continue.

Christopher Eve
Elder Son

* * *

I WAS VERY LUCKY   CATHY EVE

One of my earliest memories is of dad coming to rescue me from a nightmare. Lions were coming through my bedroom walls and he came in with his fencing sword and fought them off. Dad was my hero and I firmly believed his bed-time stories of piracy and told my friends that my dad had been a pirate and had caught a whale.

Whenever I think about dad, I think about *Privateer* and the exciting and unusual holidays we had on her. Dad always made my friends welcome and we had a lot of fun, which began with wading through mud to get to the dinghy from the sea-wall. We then had to wash the mud off so that none of it would be transferred to the pristine decks. Getting aboard was really quite an achievement! *Privateer* always seemed to need barnacles scraping off and dad did his utmost to make it a fun thing to do. If there was a pub within a couple of miles, dad would happily row against the wind and tide and take everybody for a drink. Food, until Pat came along, was all out of tins - stew was a favourite and a whole chicken a delicacy - but tasted delicious after a day at sea. In the evening the cabin was always cosy in the light of the Tilley lamp and we'd often have a game of bridge. At night we would crawl into our sleeping bags and hope it wouldn't rain, because the only bunk that didn't get dripped on was the captain's.

Dad may have had the best bunk, but he didn't always get the best deal. He often reminded me of the time we sailed to Osea Island together, when I was about six. We unpacked the picnic and found three hard-boiled eggs. I was the one who ate two.

Dad was always cool, calm and collected on land. If another driver did something stupid he would open the window and say 'Twit' and calmly drive on. On the boat we used to see another side of him. He would get exasperated when a land-lubber, like myself, couldn't understand a nautical instruction and instead of explaining what he wanted us to do he would keep shouting the same command. The crew always had fun teasing him about it afterwards. I think we were all glad to see that emotions could sometimes get out of control and break through the cool exterior that he usually presented to the world.

It was in my teenage years that dad became especially important to me. We used to spend a lot of time discussing everything and I was tremendously proud of his communist background and work on the Left at that time when we were all demonstrating for a better world. There seemed to be very little generation gap and my friends would come along to his parties.

When I became involved in Greece dad shared my enthusiasm and we always exchanged long letters. We used to talk about bringing *Privateer* out to Greece, but there was never enough time for such a big project.

After dad became ill twelve years ago, he always showed extraordinary strength in the face of adversity. He never complained but carried out doctors' orders and made the best of it. Thanks to Pat he was able to continue nearly all his pursuits. Luckily his mind was never affected and he seemed to retain everything, thus earning himself the title of 'walking encyclopaedia'.

I'm going to miss him terribly, but I think I was very lucky to have had him for a father and to have been so close to him.

Cathy Eve
Daughter

* * *

YOUR WARM SMILE   WILL EVE

I remember your smile, never far away from your lips, and your warm embrace always ready to comfort me at four years old or forty. My strongest childhood memories are of spending time with you on the boat, sometimes going far away, sometimes just 'ditch crawling'. I know this meant a lot to you, as well as to me.

You seemed to get happier as you got older, despite your physical afflictions. I hope you were not hiding too much of your physical suffering from us. You have given a lot to Cathy, Emilie, François, Annie, Marianne and me, we will not forget you. I like to think that the part of you that lives on in us is that warm smile.

Will Eve
Younger son

* * *

FROM SAILING A BOAT TO   LAURIE EVE
EUROPEAN HISTORY

What I shared with grandad was somewhere between a grandfather-grandson, and a father-son relationship.

He has been a huge part of my life, giving me invaluable support, encouragement, and an insight into a better future.

As with most people, I would not say that my life has been easy, but every moment I spent with grandad made me forget about any troubles - everything simply felt great whenever I was around him. These are some of the happiest times, the happiest memories, I have, especially aboard *Privateer*, where he 'toughened' me up for anything! Every moment I spent with him was so special that I cannot single out any one memory as an example. He taught me so much about anything and everything, from sailing a boat to European history. I was always amazed at how grandad seemed to know just about everything!

He is my hero; the most courageous man I have ever known. The way he coped with his disabilities was astounding; never once did he complain or so much as show a sad face. In fact, he frequently sang to me 'always look on the bright side of life,' which I think just about sums up his light-heartedness. He did not just get along with life, he excelled in life, endlessly achieving. I could not desire a better role model.

Grandad has left me inspired; inspired to achieve any goals I set against any odds that may be.

I am privileged to have such a great man, such a courageous man, such a brilliant intellectual, such a great teacher, as my grandfather.

In loving memory from a loving grandson and crew.

Laurie Eve
Grandson
                    * * *

MERLIN PRESS: EARLY YEARS

EARLY BEGINNINGS

MARTIN EVE

Merlin was born on the 27th of July 1956, with the publication of our first book.

The book and its author were both somewhat unusual. The author had been an early member of the SDF and had become a monk for 10 years in the Anglican church; when the whole monastery went over to Rome, George Chambers was appointed a curate, first in Thaxted and then given a parish of his own in Norfolk.

He was a founder member of the Communist Party; he had always been a very keen folklorist. He had worked with Cecil Sharp in the early days of folksong, but in his career in the church, had become something of a classicist, with a special interest in early church music. What his book *Folksong-Plainsong* did was to address the problem of musical origins. Did folk music, as was almost universally believed at that time, originate as a vulgarisation or adaptation of church music; or, as folksingers believed, was it the other way round?

George Chambers was able to use classical sources to show how the early church had deliberately taken and adapted popular songs so that the congregations would be able to join in with tunes that they knew using the church's new words for them.

There was much comparison between some early versions of Plainsong with folk tunes, especially from the Appalachians, but from other parts of the world as well. As a book, it was difficult, first because folksingers were not interested in the classical side, while composers of church music were not interested in folksong. There was also some difficulty, in those days before photolitho was in use, in actually setting Plainsong notation (this last difficulty was solved by finding a nunnery in Berkshire where they would do this and make the blocks).

How this book came to me was as follows. The publisher, Dennis Dobson, who was a friend also of George Chambers, and deeply interested in music, had accepted it. Dennis Dobson ran an ambitious publishing programme on a shoestring and every now and then had a financial crisis. These were normally solved by a timely visit to one of his many aunts, who normally came up with what was needed. On this occasion, however, the aunts let him down and Dobson was obliged to send back the typescript to George Chambers and say that he could not undertake to publish it.

At this time, I was working as the West Country representative for Michael Joseph and I had plans, of a sort, to enter publishing, which I thought I might be able to do by finding a partner with some money and no experience, while I could supply the opposite. My experience as a representative, first freelancing for small firms, (these included Weidenfeld and Nicolson and Harvill Press, amongst others) and later, with the more prestigious Michael Joseph, had given me a considerable insight into selling books.

I had made one or two approaches, but had been unable to get anywhere near a suitable partner for my project. When Father George Chambers' book was put in front of me, I felt that I must do something for an old friend and I would publish it myself. I knew nothing of the production process and what was needed, but I made it my business to find out, although it took a long time to produce. This was due to several things.

One of them was that Father George had a tendency to turn up, quite frequently, with some new material gleaned from new researches, which had to be fitted in. Eventually we brought out the book, in a reasonably acceptable form, and sent out the review copies.

We had first secured a short Foreword by Vaughan Williams, in which he referred to 'bat eyed musicologists'. This ensured us an extremely hostile press from all the musicologists who, in those days, ran a surprising number of musical journals. We did, however, have one favourable review from *The Times*' musical correspondent and, of course, we had the support of the English Folksong and Dance Society.

Rarely did a book receive so much individual attention; fliers were sent out everywhere and bookshops were canvassed to take the odd copy. But the controversial nature of the book, which nowadays might perhaps lead to a silent demise, in those days lead to at least some sales and it became clear fairly soon that the book had established a small place in the market and would sell.

This encouraged me to think that if such an extremely difficult book, with everything running against it, could be sold, then almost anything else would be easy going. I was still working for Michael Joseph, by now as London rep, but it was clear that it would be difficult to go on with the job and start a publishing house at the same time. I had told them about *Folksong-Plainsong*; when I had a copy to show them I gave in my notice, which I do not think came as any surprise to them.

I had meanwhile been trying to get together some other new books, so that Merlin would not be a one book publisher for longer than necessary. Before I come to these, I will have to make a digression in the way of autobiography, to explain how I came to be in the position of wanting to start up or join in with a left-wing publisher.

The story starts with family influences, where my mother had always been a Christian Socialist of a very practical sort and was for many years a Labour Councillor in Suffolk where we lived. Partly as a result of this, partly the luck of the draw, I managed to get a scholarship to Bryanston, where I was in contact with Marxist ideas.

Bryanston, classed as a public school, was quite remarkable if not unique. The whole ethos of the school was entirely contrary to that of any other public school; it was cooperative and not competitive. We had no class order or marking to discriminate between one boy and another. The only competition was with yourself and what you were capable of. There were competitive games, but everyone joined in for enjoyment rather than from an obsession with winning.

The staff was evenly divided between communists and pacifists. While respecting some of the pacifists, who included Aubrey de Selincourt who taught me English, I tended to take more notice of the communists who included my housemaster, Wilfred Cowley; who when I arrived at the school, sat me in the library and gave me a copy of Claud Cockburn's Spanish Cockpit to read. I also began to read the latest Left Book Club issues and borrowed two books (in succession) from the library. One was Adam Smith's *Wealth of Nations* and the other was Marx's *Capital*, which I found more difficult to follow; but I think I got the general idea.

We had political discussion groups of every sort and I was soon in an unofficial grouping of lefties, where we spoke of the Chamberlain appeasement policies with disgust and where we all thought the Soviet Union was on the side of the angels.

I recall that the school, which had never had an OTC, responded to the outbreak of war by starting up an Air Training Corps, which most of us joined. Like almost everything in the school, it was not compulsory. Marching off to our classes in signalling, navigation or whatever, there were enough of us to get a left-wing song going as we marched.

When the Soviet Union was dragged into the war on my 17th birthday, June 22nd 1941, I knew what I wanted to do. I had some nautical background, my father being quite a well-known yachtsman in his day, and I wanted to get into the Navy. I was not going to wait patiently for my 18th birthday but falsified my age and went off for training as an ordinary seaman when still 17. Experience on the lower deck (of a corvette in the Atlantic) introduced me for the first time to the British working class. Previously, all my socialist ideas had been entirely theoretical but I now confronted ordinary people, nearly all volunteers, and they were broadminded enough to accept me into their lives and conversations, in a very open way, despite my upper class accent.

My acceptance was helped by two things; I was willing to spend afternoons making huge suet puddings for my messmates (they were known as 'Lofty's duffs'), and later when I was fortunate enough to be able to get a line round one of the crew who had fallen overboard, fortunately in the warm waters of the Mediterranean.

I developed a profound respect for the very different ideas on life of these sailors and I think my subsequent commitment to Socialism owed more to my feelings of solidarity with them than with any collection of theoretical ideas, however attractive these were to me later.

On my return from the Mediterranean I said goodbye to my shipmates and after due course emerged as a very young naval officer. This is not entirely irrelevant to what followed, as serving three years as an overpaid officer with practically no opportunities of spending any of my pay, left me with a substantial nest egg at the end of the war.

On demobilisation, a grateful government sent me to Cambridge where I studied History with a lot of enthusiasm, and joined the Cambridge student Communist Party group; at that time about fifty members and not a shadow of its glory days in the thirties.

Another member of this group was Edward Thompson who was in my College and a friend from early days. After I had graduated, I had been hoping to follow Edward as a WEA Lecturer. I had been doing a bit of this part time in the evenings and expected to be able to pick up a full time job somewhere. Unfortunately my College, willing to give me a good reference in all other ways, ended it by saying; 'We feel it our duty to tell you that this student is an active member of the Communist Party'. Which was, of course, true, but in 1950 absolutely devastating for any hopes of a job.

I tried every way of getting round this difficulty but it was hard to explain why I wasn't giving a reference after being at College for three years. To keep body and soul together, I got a very satisfactory job on a building site in Dulwich, near to where I was in digs and where the foreman soon recognised me as a reliable worker and would give me the afternoon off; I went home, put my best suit on and went off to another hopeless interview.

At this point I remembered that I had, at one time, taken quite an interest in publishing. I was friendly at school with Oliver Marston whose father had spent a lifetime in publishing and quite a bit of background knowledge filtered through to me.

I was also friendly with Kenneth Ingram who, apart from writing, had a part interest in a very small publishing house called Quality Press. This was the contact that I used to get an interview with the employment agency then run by The Publishers' Association. I had already taken the trouble to read Sir Stanley Unwin's masterly treatise on publishing, *The Truth*, and was one of the few people I know of in those days, who actually followed his advice to enter publishing via a job as a representative. He had sent his eldest son Rayner to do this when very young and anyway it was advice that I took and with good results. I very quickly picked up a freelance job with Harvill Press who found another group of publishers to make up about half a dozen. After a short probation in the London suburbs, I was despatched to Bristol to represent them. One of this half a dozen was a very small firm called Weidenfeld and Nicolson. I found it very difficult to sell their literary productions in the West Country and resigned to replace them with another publisher. I did this for two years and it was an invaluable experience. I was able to absorb the knowledge and experience of all the West Country booksellers and to see the sort of problems faced by a small publisher.

On the strength of these two years, I got an exclusive job in the same area for Michael Joseph, a very go-ahead producer of bestsellers, (the current ones then were the Doctor books), and who published C.S. Forester, Monica Dickens and many other best-selling writers. This was a very different experience and I now knew what it was like to surf on the crest of a wave of commercial success.

It was during this time that the first glimmerings of the idea of the, as yet unnamed Merlin, were beginning to come into existence. When Michael Joseph offered me a job in London, I jumped at the opportunity; in those days it was impossible for any publisher to operate anywhere else. I did another two years for Michael Joseph in London, which were not so happy. There was more bustle and less literary talk and it took me a long time to get used to the very different scene there.

This was my publishing experience when I jumped into the deep end in 1956. Politically, I was becoming a less and less enthusiastic member of the Communist Party: still doing work for them but very critical of what was slowly emerging from Russia. When the Khrushchev speech was first published it had the same devastating effect on me as on every other Communist; early on I determined that if our British Party could not accept these criticisms and adapt accordingly, that it was no place to be. So the starting of Merlin caught me at a turning point in my political ideas as well as a turning point for all the Left. Instead of acting as a sort of literary supplement to the, at that time, extremely narrow and dull political party publisher, Lawrence and Wishart, it was clear that my role would be with the New Left. I pursued this in various ways through the early New Left organisations and also by opening files on two continental Marxists: one Berthold Brecht and the other Georg Lukács.

The file on Brecht increased in size and led to some encouraging meetings but no more. The Lukács file, with the help of István Mészáros, began a long correspondence with Lukács as soon as he was released from his Romanian prison and bore fruit in *The Historical Novel* first published in 1962.

Of course, I needed to get a list together quickly and this was a difficult problem. Even if you can persuade authors to write books for you it takes time. To get things started I looked to get some translations going as soon as I could.

I was very fortunate in having the friendship of Jonathan and Frieda Knight. Jonathan was a professor of Microbiology but also a natural translator from the French and an expert on Stendhal. Following the war, there had been a shortage of translations of classical authors. Before the war, cultured readers could be expected to read French, though not perhaps Russian or German. This was no longer the case and so I commissioned two Stendhal translations: the first, *The Life of Henry Brulard*, was an autobiographical book which had never been published before in Britain, though a shortened version had appeared in America. This was an astonishing omission; it is a brilliant book full of insights, which carried a contemporary relevance; it is hard to remember it was written in the early part of the 19th century. The other was the rather more popular, perhaps, *de L'Amour*, which had appeared in a translation by Vyvyan Holland, but had been long out of print

Jonathan Knight oversaw both translations and encouraged me to commission the new one for the *de L'Amour*. *Henry Brulard*, when it came out was, I can only say, a literary success. It had the lead reviews on the two Sundays, *The Times* and *Observer*, and elsewhere it was a Book Society recommendation, widely acclaimed in particular for the quality of the translation. In due course, *Love* when it was published did not receive quite such a critical welcome, but a very valuable boost was given by a highly favourable review by the journalist Nancy Spain. In fact, if *Henry Brulard* was a critical success, *Love* was much more of a commercial success and the London bookshops were reordering half a dozen at a time.

Very many years later, I persuaded Penguin to do a paperback of both books; they kept *Henry Brulard* in print for many years and still keep *Love* going. This gave me a great deal of confidence to proceed with other things and I published my first green book called *Lands Alive* by Rene Dumont, the French environmentalist. At that time none of his work had been translated and he was not widely known, but the book was in fact accepted in the specialised academic world, and we reasonably soon sold out a modest edition.

I was hoping to be able to turn away from translations to original work as soon as possible. One of the problems I had was that I had insufficient money and follow-up success. I couldn't afford to translate any more Rene Dumont for the moment and his next book *Black Africa is Off to a Bad Start*, was a tremendous success published by Deutsch and was compulsory reading for the new rulers of former Colonial Africa.

This was the fate of several other projects. For instance, later on I published a translation of *Totemism* by Levi-Strauss, but could not follow this with a far more important work of his. Meanwhile, all my resources were being put into the publication of a major project, originally suggested to me by Ralph Miliband. The original of Ernest Mandel's *Marxist Economic Theory* had been passed over by several English publishing houses. His French publisher had given up hoping for an English translation and, after some scepticism that I would be able to handle this 800 page work, agreed to give me a contract. This strained resources very greatly; the book was being translated in longhand by Brian Pearce, who meticulously checked all the quotations and frequently wrote to Mandel, asking him to look up the originals which he could not find. Although Mandel was obviously grateful to have the errors corrected and eventually made our edition the authoritative edition rather than his own French one, I do think he must have resented these monthly inquisitions which showed shortcomings in his research. The longhand, when checked, had to be typed elsewhere and then in the methods of printing employed in those days be set in galleys, checked by Brian and by me and then stockpiled until we had reached the final page and could do the index. The whole operation from start to finish took four years.

Early on in these years there was a significant development and I will come to this next. In the *New Statesman*, Hugh Burnett, a BBC producer responsible for 'Face To Face' and other programmes, was drawing cartoons of monks in various situations; these seemed to me to be worth collecting and publishing in a small cheap edition containing 30 to 40 drawings. I brought these out with the title *Top Sacred* in 1960 and it was an instant success. Very quickly it was through three or four printings, and every year we produced a new volume. An added bonus was that we sold rights in U.S.A. and Holland and eventually English paperback rights when we felt we had done all we could.

The success of 'The monks' had a considerable effect on Merlin in lots of ways. It gave us a foothold in bookshops. It took away the weight of never losing money on a book and ensuring that every single one was a success, and it was a regular source of income for many years with foreign rights as well as the relatively small turnover on a cheap book. The advantage that I was now able to make a mistake without it proving fatal did not in fact alter the habit of being very discriminating about what was published.

I think this is the point at which I have to confess my difficulties in writing a history of Merlin. I had never kept a publishers' daily diary, but I had kept a scrapbook archive, which gave all the information. This was lost in the course of two quick moves in the late 1980s and therefore I am having to work on memory, helped of course by the presence of a complete set of all the books that we ever published.

It was proving more difficult than I had expected to get into the New Left of this country as a publisher. In fact long before I did so I had published a collection of translated Polish pieces, including one by the dissident Marxist Colkovsky entitled *The Broken Mirror*. Fortunately it was a joint project with the American publishers and it was not a financial disaster that despite reviews I was only able to sell 300 copies.

The New Left had got off to quite a promising start with *The New Reasoner* and then the new wave of younger people represented by *Universities and Left Review*. However, that *Broken Mirror* statistic does show that there had been a dwindling of the numbers of people who defected from the Communist Party in 1956 or 1957, roughly 10,000 men and women, that evidently fewer and fewer continued to take an interest in Left politics.

The formation of *New Left Review* as a fusion between *The New Reasoner* and *Universities and Left Review* did begin a revival, which brought in new people and not the 'relics' of the Communist Party alone.

At one time we were handling *New Left Review* for the bookshops but I had still not been able to get together an equivalent book.

Meanwhile the translations of Lukács and later of Mandel were at last beginning to show up as completely translated books and were beginning to establish a reputation in this publishing niche. It was not until the split up of the original team for *New Left Review* in 1963, well documented by Thompson, (see *Socialist Register* 1965), which opened up an opportunity. Ralph Miliband and John Saville had originally hoped to incorporate Edward Thompson as one of the editors of a new journal to appear annually. Thompson, however, while giving full support and contributing articles to many of the issues, had been exhausted by the editorship of *The New Reasoner* and did not feel he could take on another such assignment. As all his friends would know, he was not somebody who would take on something like this without throwing himself into it wholeheartedly and this he did not feel able to do.

The project was discussed in 1963 and I did suggest that *Register* would be better as a title than the traditional *Socialist Review*, of which there had been several in the past and were to be more in the future in both Britain and America. The title, borrowed of course from Cobbett, has stuck and so has the magazine *New Left Review* which has lasted very much longer than the majority of left wing periodicals and shows no sign of declining.

We were greatly helped by the active co-operation of Monthly Review Press, then under the direction of Leo Hugerman, who took a large number of the first two issues

Martin Eve

* * *

A DEAR FRIEND

IAN KIEK

I first met Martin shortly after he came down from Cambridge and had joined Michael Joseph. I believe that the year was 1953. In a very little time we became great friends and that is how it has been for over half a century.

I sensed that Martin was a very gifted person and would not remain at Michael Joseph. We would so often have lunch in the restaurant at Friends' House when we talked about the world of publishing.

In 1956 Merlin Press came into being and I recall that the first book that Martin published was *Folksong - Plainsong*. I was unaware at that time of Martin's great love of music, or that he was a considerable pianist.

All through the years of my publishing activities I kept in touch with clever Martin, and he with me. I remember so clearly while we were having lunch he showed me a cartoon in the *New Statesman* by Hugh Burnett of two monks in earnest conversation. I felt at once that a little book of Hugh Burnett's monks would have a considerable sale. Martin wrote at once to Hugh Burnett and a year later *Top Sacred* was published, quickly followed by *Sacred and Confidential* and three other monk titles. Many thousands were sold thus helping Martin to publish the books that he wished to publish.

I watched Martin with delight grow into a considerable Left wing publisher with some wonderful authors on his list including, I recall, the *Loom of Language* and *Mathematics for the Million*, originally published by Allen and Unwin. I will always treasure the copy he gave me of *An Old Gaffer's Tale* which was published in 1984 and inscribed 'For Ian - with gratitude for thirty years of friendship'.

I will always remember Martin as a dear friend, and for his great physical courage, who in 1991 drove with considerable difficulty to Worthing where I was in hospital with a broken neck after a car accident, but of course that was Martin.

His voice, his laughter and his smile will always be with me as long as I live.

Ian Kiek
Friend, publishers' representative
                                        * * *

MEMORIES OF MARTIN EVE   IAN NORRIE

Martin grew into the concrete jungle of contemporary publishing as vibrantly as any plant poking its insidious head upwards. Unlike a plant he was aware of the dangers of decapitation but had implicit faith in his roots. Somehow the modest list starting uncontroversially with *Folksong-Plainsong*, spread its unlikely tendrils to spawn *Socialist Register* - not just an annual, a perennial - and flowered in unsuspected glades, nurturing amorous volumes by Stendhal, cartoons by Hugh Burnett (depicting monks in unholy contexts) and essays by a Hungarian Marxist.

Writing about Merlin in its early days, in a journal long defunct, I attempted to investigate the financial foundation of this hardy growth. Martin smiled enigmatically, telling me he had been a naval officer and then a rep for Michael Joseph. He had a wife and three children; was a committed socialist. None of which explained how the family survived on the Merlin output.

I settled for accepting him as an eccentric. I was a bookseller; he a publisher. He not only wanted me to sell his books; he was willing to face me on a tennis court. We both liked theatre so we made a foursome and took our wives to see *Beyond the Fringe*, starring another foursome (including Alan Bennett and Jonathan Miller) who changed the face of revue forever. Martin was always beyond the fringe in publishing terms. I was mainstream in bookselling but, operating in Hampstead, I could accommodate Merlin as well as the Establishment.

Martin's publishing was conducted from two mega-cupboards knocked into one on the mezzanine floor of a Victorian house on the corner of Fitzroy Square. From there emanated such organisation as he thought necessary. Later he moved to the Isle of Dogs where I refused to visit him in case he served his home brewed beer. Years after he occupied two floors in Malden Road, Kentish Town. They were more spacious though no less unkempt than the Fitzrovian wardrobe. Here he was joined by Norman Franklin who had owned and sold a major imprint, exchanging a battleship for Martin's tramp steamer. It didn't work. How could it? In the world Norman had vacated the process of publishing was differently approached. Martin explained – 'When a typescript came in, Norman would say, "Who shall we ask to read it?" I would reply, "Why don't we read it ourselves?"'. They parted amicably.

On the tennis court Martin recognised the need for a racket and balls. For footwear he used whatever he had on at the time. There was no question of changing into a tennis shirt and shorts. He was not noted for sartorial elegance on any occasion. Yet he took his game seriously. All his determination to fight for any cause seemingly lost, often made him victor.

In those pre-tiebreak days we would reach six-all, only to conclude, 22-20, or 16-14, in his favour. He recognised neither bad light nor snow as adverse playing conditions. At Konigstein, during a visit to the Frankfurt Book Fair, we played long after dark had descended; in Finchley, where the court bore evidence of overnight blizzards, I once faced his serve with fingers frozen to my racket.

At Frankfurt, Martin hired a small stand without embellishments. On our only visit in 1968 Mavis and I attempted to decorate it, to make it look as attractive as other publishers' stands. It was the only year that Martin failed to conclude any deals.

Between marriages Martin lived in a bedsit in Highgate, where a pulsating fridge stood next to his bed. As an ex-sailor this did not bother him. Also, as an old seadog, he published books about sailing without, so far as I know, any political leanings, but I daresay they veered to port.

There was an element of fanaticism in Martin's beliefs but it was offset by an overall humour, humanity and a devotion to scholarship. Also, some pride in the fact that he had never sold out.

Ian Norrie
Bookseller

* * *

SOCIALIST REGISTER

FIRST VOLUME AND BEYOND

MARION KOZAK

My friendship with Martin dates back to the very first volume of *Socialist Register*, co-edited by Ralph Miliband until his death in 1994, and Martin is therefore associated with the 60s and the events of that period. We saw a lot of Martin at the time, fetching and carrying proofs which went into galleys first, interminably long reels of paper which hung over the desk in an antique fashion, as in 30s movies. Later galleys disappeared and the *Register* went from typescript directly into page-proof, to Ralph's consternation, since he knew that the new system would not allow him substantive changes after he had finally let go of a manuscript. We talked a lot of politics and history with Martin and I was always amazed by his knowledge of neglected Left causes such as the civil war in Greece, the fate of Dubcek's Czechoslovakia, and the subsequent repression whose victims were washed up on these shores like so much flotsam. It was real live politics that inspired Martin to publish some of the books on Merlin's list such as Marian Sling's and Marion Sarafis' memoirs of traumatic experiences in Czechoslovakia and Greece. Martin had a healthy dislike of the abuse of power, whether it was lodged in the secret services, the military, or even in the seat of legitimate civil government or among grasping publishers. He relished being a small publishing outfit with a small amount of power to publish what he wholeheartedly approved of and, on at least one occasion, he made a point of offering employment to a civil servant, on her release from jail, who had revealed some uncomfortable home truths about our government's policies in the 80s.

I always enjoyed Martin's comings and goings; his offering of odd and fascinating historical bits of information. On Monday evenings, he sometimes came by with loads of galleys and a bowlful of oysters picked up on his weekend sailing trips. I became quite expert at opening these craggy creatures with a rusty old penknife which has since disappeared but the blue/white striped bowl, stayed with us for years.

Martin was always fascinated by the sea. It was only much later that I picked up some of his deep feelings, inherited partly from the time that his father was setting up oyster beds in Orford. Martin remembered being carried as a child on his father's shoulders, seeing herds of porpoises and seals on the Suffolk coast, creatures now rarely seen. The sea was part of his childhood and also of his young adulthood. When I last saw him he told me about his volunteering for the navy during the war, his service as a rating and later an officer. He clearly relished reminiscing about this period of his life, which turned out to be a transforming, political experience. I marvelled at the vividness of the detail and how, despite his illness, he managed to say so much about his mates, his friendships and his own place in that dangerous and unfamiliar wartime jigsaw. That last meeting is my abiding memory of Martin.

Marion Kozak
Friend, wife of first editor, *Socialist Register* supporter
* * *

FAREWELL SERVICE ADDRESS   LEO PANITCH

When Martin said farewell to me on a transatlantic telephone call a few days before he died, and asked me to come over and speak at his funeral, he also expressed his sense of fulfilment at having shared, as he put it, in our socialist-humanist project. He was referring, of course, to our work together on the *Socialist Register*, of which I had been co-editor only since 1985, but which Martin's Merlin Press had been the publisher of since its inception thirty-five years ago. Indeed, soon after this annual volume of essays was conceived by its two founding editors, Ralph Miliband and John Saville, at a meeting in 1963 with Martin's close friend and comrade, Edward Thompson, it was Martin who came up with the title *Socialist Register*, brought to mind by Thompson's account of Cobden's Annual Register in his *Making of the English Working Class*. Along with other books he published in the 1960s and 1970s, Martin thereby made an enormous contribution to the renewal of Marxist ideas and democratic socialist politics to which Martin and comrades had committed themselves when they left the Communist Party after 1956.

The first time I met Martin in the mid 1980s, I recall very clearly thinking what a remarkable man he was as I watched him leaving Ralph Miliband and Marion Kozak's house, his feet and hands already handicapped, slowly and deliberately putting on his helmet, mounting his motorbike and driving off waving and smiling as if it was the most natural thing for a man with his handicaps to do. As we worked together so closely over the ensuing years, I came not only to rely on his brilliant editing skills, but also on his wit, his judgement, his support and his encouragement for each and every volume of the *Register*. Indeed his role grew rather than diminished through the 1990s. It was Martin's unflagging enthusiasm that often kept me going, and I know that he in turn derived a great deal of satisfaction from knowing that the *Register* was reaching a new generation, as when in the last few years he arranged for an Indian Edition, or when he heard that articles from the *Register* were being translated and circulated by socialist dissidents in China and Iran.

In the last year of his life, Martin put a great deal of effort into the preparation of two volumes of the *Register*. He was especially excited that the 1998 volume was devoted to essays on *The Communist Manifesto Now*; it was his idea to include the *Manifesto* itself in the volume; and he enthusiastically sponsored the marvellous evening of celebration of the *Manifesto*'s 150th anniversary organised by Sheila Rowbotham and Dave Timms at London's Conway Hall last May, sending a message to be read there although he could not travel to attend. Right up to the last he worked on the proofs for the 1999 volume on the theme of *Global Capitalism versus Democracy* and was pleased and moved that it was being dedicated to him.

Martin's legacy will live on. He was determined in the last weeks to try to ensure that Merlin and the *Register* would continue in good hands. But he shall be missed very much. Colin Leys, who has joined me as co-editor and who worked closely with Martin over the past 18 months, put it very aptly in a note he sent me the day he learned of Martin's death. 'He was an example of something I seem to increasingly miss - unswerving adherence to principle, indifference to material things, total lack of deference to the rich and powerful, a broad and deep culture. It has affected me more than I imagined, especially his courage in face of his death.'

I am acutely aware that it was one of the great privileges of my life to have known and worked with Martin Eve.

Leo Panitch
Editor *Socialist Register*

* * *

LIFE AT MERLIN PRESS

I'LL MISS HIM   LOUIS MACKAY

When I first knew Martin, twenty years ago, Merlin had a draughty office down in what the developers, as soon as the last few ships had discharged their timber, would soon be calling 'Docklands'. Though the river had an appealing Dickensian ambience, it was a run-down area, and the graffiti someone had added to the sign as you turned south along Manchester Road has stuck in my memory: '*you're* WELCOME TO THE ISLE OF DOGS, *it's the shits!*' Martin used to turn up on a small motorbike - on which, I seem to remember, he once rode to Frankfurt with a box of his best titles for the Book Fair. We would walk through the foot-tunnel to Greenwich for a pie and a pint in the pub, and natter about politics, history, and the sea.

At a time when independent publishers were fast being destroyed or devoured by ever vaster publishing conglomerates, it was refreshing to find that anyone could keep an outfit like Merlin going - and Martin could, helped by a good list, a Spartan indifference to uncomfortable conditions (not shared in quite the same measure by all who worked for him), and, well, a knack for avoiding extravagance.

Away from Limehouse Reach, two particularly vivid images of Martin in his element remain in my mind. One is from the heyday of END, with Edward Thompson and others at evening meetings of an ad hoc 'publications committee,' where both the old friendship, and the common ground that Edward and Martin had shared were still very evident. There were of course many other dynamics, but I have no doubt that Martin, as Edward's publisher, helped in a real way to loosen the mental concrete that the Cold War had been staged on for a generation, west and east of the Elbe. The fact that the world has moved into different and scarcely less dangerous crises in no way diminishes the gratitude we owe them both for that.

My other indelible image is of Martin at the helm of *Privateer*. It probably struck many people as unusual to find a socialist with such a love of sailing. Through Seafarer books, Martin illuminated popular and democratic strands in Britain's maritime culture that are too often obscured by the stereotypes of Cowes week - and gave life to some good yarns while he was about it.

He was interested in topics that had come my way from doing bits of Scandinavian translation for the National Maritime Museum - mostly concerning either the last days of commercial sail, or dark age maritime archaeology - a field into which Merlin had ventured with Charles

Green's *Sutton Hoo*, and its experiential insights into the routes Saxon migrants rowed in their crossings. Martin had tried some of them himself, with the benefit of sails, in *Privateer*.

It was a treat to be invited sailing in the old gaffer. We crossed the Thames estuary from Sheppey in a fine summer breeze, and spent a night beached on Osea island, talking late in the dim lamplight with the waders piping across the marshes and the rising tide lapping at the hull.

I won't forget another, livelier, sail, some years later, when we ran into a line of increasingly violent squalls. Behind the squalls came seven eighths of a gale, in which we soon lost sight of the Essex coast. The sea turned vicious, ripped the steel gallows off the deck, robbed us of the dinghy we were towing and made some grabs at the crew. The boat was shipping water from waves breaking over the bow. Pat and I were busy bailing buckets of sea from the cabin and, as the light began to fade, the foolish thought that we might have been in trouble crossed my mind, fleetingly.

One glance at the skipper, quite unruffled as he steered in the general direction of England, was enough to dispel that. And, before long, we were in quieter water, chasing a coaster into Brightlingsea harbour.

Even then, nearly ten years ago, Martin was already quite badly disabled. But he had the tiller jammed under his arm and Cape Horn wouldn't have shaken him off it. The same good-humoured tenacity governed his attachment to life - his determination not to let his illness grind him down. The same confident assurance characterised a radical consciousness that lived on in him, not as ideology, but as the caulking in his planks.

I don't know how he managed it. He must have struggled more than he wanted people to know, especially in later years. The lasting memory that all who knew him must have of him is of a brave and admirable man, tough as cable.

I'll miss him.

Louis Mackay
Jacket Designer

* * *

LONG LIVE MERLIN! BILL NORRIS

A man with a grin and a battered motorcycle helmet raps on the window of 37 Grays Inn Road, home of Central Books, just after the last customer has left. It's a publisher delivering books in person for an order taken earlier that day by the representative of Merlin Press. It's Martin Eve, saving money on delivery costs and providing a fast friendly service - I didn't know it then but he probably packed the parcel as well. Of course, he stops for a quick chat and a word of encouragement. It's 1975 and I'm new to bookselling and publishing but I quickly realise that this is not normal publisher behaviour, but it's typically Martin.

A few weeks later I am asked to go down to a warehouse on the Isle of Dogs, pre-Canary Wharf, pre-Thatcher, this really feels like an island with old industrial wharfs and warehouses fronting the river and a feeling of an older London scene. In the process of manhandling Soviet boxes of the *Collected Works* of Marx and Engels I discover that Martin is the controller of what seems to me a vast emporium of radical literature, not just his Merlin Press but other American publishers. Hundreds of titles all neatly laid out in the kind of quantities I have never seen before, this is my first view of a publisher's warehouse. Somewhere I think in the middle of this warehouse is a kind of office where books are invoiced, orders processed and phones ring. I begin to piece together the world of a publisher who seems to do everything from commission, edit, store, sell, pack and deliver his books. Of course he has helpers and co-workers, but I have the feeling that not much escapes his attention. I must stress that Martin showed the comradely good business sense to charge Central Books for storage for many books that proved very hard to sell (over twenty years later some of them still lie in deep storage in our warehouse).

Many years later, nearly ten years ago, I persuaded Martin to somewhat reverse our earlier relations. This time round, Central Books took in the considerable inventory of Merlin, Greenprint and Seafarer. Of course Martin being Martin, he was adamant that there would be no storage charges! All my earlier impressions that Martin was a 'hands on' publisher were fully confirmed. Some publishers keep sales and stock reports for a rainy day, the Merlin approach was always to examine them carefully, and immediately deal with all apparent anomalies. Weekly conversations with Martin would range from current politics, the mystery of missing stocks, print runs and the appropriate price for his next title. Preparing and sending out Merlin sales reports with no Martin at the other end to read, digest and respond is strange. Despite his sometimes sharp response to unwelcome sales data and his eagle eye for stock problems I would love to have him at the other end of the phone keeping us on our toes. Goodbye Martin; Long live Merlin!

Bill Norris
Comrade, Central Books

* * *

FITZROY SQUARE   TINA CRAIG

When I started work at the Merlin Press in the spring of 1969 it was my first 'proper job' since graduating the previous summer. I had written round to innumerable publishers without success and it was my great good fortune that Martin's secretary had just resigned and Martin was about to put an advert in *The Bookseller* when my letter arrived! I don't know what I expected of 'a career in publishing' and Martin must certainly have regretted not giving me a typing test (my only claim to secretarial skills was based on a rudimentary 'Sight and Sound Course'), but we spent three years working together in a tiny little office up some steep stone stairs in Fitzroy Square and had some amazing times!

Martin was a wonderful boss. Charming, sociable and enthusiastic; he worked hard himself and expected the same of his staff. But the day did not really start until a mug or two of strong coffee had been made and *The Times* crossword conquered. Fascinating people often dropped by for a chat and, of course, there were endless discussions on the political events of the day. If sales had been good or a promising new author signed up there would be a celebratory meal in one of the numerous local curry houses. When István Mészáros' great work finally came out and we had to work long hours, Martin gave me some extra money (I was, of course, always paid in cash) with which I bought an outfit I always thought of as my *History and Class Consciousness* dress! Running the Press on a shoe-string, Martin was always a bit of a 'wheeler-dealer'. He drove a battered old Citroën Safari for which it was hard to get parts and was delighted when he met someone selling a similar model - for years he drove round with 2 spare doors in the back 'in case they came in useful'! When the mast on his boat needed replacing at vast cost he was delighted to discover a man selling old telegraph poles and used to tell the story of going to select one from huge piles of the things!

Then there was *Privateer*. Arriving in the office on sunny summer Mondays, I never knew whether Martin would be present or if there would be a message from some obscure destination or other claiming unavoidable delays due to lack of wind or tide etc. I had some delightful trips with Martin and various friends on his beloved boat - once I had steeled myself to the 'bucket on deck' facilities - and he was very tolerant, under the circumstances, of my hopelessness with the ropes! I shall always remember the pleasure of the first warming glass of rum after a stiff day's sailing and the sounds of the birds on the mud flats when waking in one's bunk in the morning.

Chris and I vividly remember being invited for a trip to Boulogne; we were due to meet Martin in Dover at 5am to catch the tide. Bleary eyed, we turned up, all set to embark, but a rope snagged and ended up wound around the propeller and Martin had to dive into the icy waters of the harbour to free it! Becalmed at first, we were hit by very severe weather and often unable to see the other vessels at sea. I spent most of the trip ill below decks and Chris cracked a rib when he was knocked against the bulkhead. We eventually made Calais (near enough!) - narrowly avoiding a collision with a Sealink ferry - and moored behind the original 'three men in a boat,' who cheered us up by telling us how they'd been run down by a tanker in the Medway!

I shall always remember my years at the Merlin Press. When I think of Martin now, I think of his smile, his infectious laugh and the lovely quirky way he would tell a story. On one of the last times we spoke he was explaining how failing to sell his flat on account of a cherry tree meant that he eventually sold it for considerably more - as he put it, it was a very valuable tree!

Tina Craig
Publisher's assistant

* * *

THOUGHTS OF MARTIN   SARAH TISDALL

I first came across Martin in March 1984. He wrote and offered me a job. Towards the end of my sentence my mum was despatched to see if the offer was (a) genuine and (b) still open - it was. I went for an 'interview' in August that year, following my release. The interview consisted of moving a pile of paper from one chair to another, a tour of the premises and a cup of coffee. I was sent off with E.P. Thompson's latest work and an invitation to give my opinion.

I liked the piece and so was deemed suitable material to work for Merlin.

At that time Merlin Press was based in an old coach house on the Isle of Dogs. There was a large shed at the back of the building filled with books, the ground floor was also filled with books. Upstairs there were three rooms, a library/kitchen, a room for the Augustus Kelley reprints and 'the office' - three desks, two large typewriters and a filing cabinet. There was no heating. (More of this later).

Lunch was always taken in Greenwich. We would walk through the underground tunnel to go to the pub where Martin would have a shepherd's pie and a pint, followed by a walk back through the tunnel stopping only to collect a Kit Kat for afternoon break.

There was one memorable occasion when we took the man from Coutt's on this trek and asked him to assist us in carrying some boxes back from the pub to help us with packing some books that afternoon. It was a long time before we heard from the bank after that!

The advantage of a small firm is that you can become involved in everything and I did with a lot of help from Martin. He was always asking me questions, not 'Where's that manuscript?' or 'Have we paid so and so?' but 'Yes, but what is it really about?' The answer would usually involve an analysis of class and power, which at the time was all new to me and I didn't always understand.

The Filing Cabinet

The filing cabinet was for the most part completely empty. On top of the filing cabinet there was an almost empty bottle of brandy and a mound of paper - waiting to be filed. I once found a letter dated 1964, so some of it had been there for a while. However, if we ever wanted to find something we knew where it would be - in the pile somewhere and if you could remember the year concerned then sooner or later you would find it. The bottle of brandy remained untouched until the day Clive Ponting was found not guilty and we took the opportunity to have a sip each and finish the bottle.

Heating

The building was so cold we would type out invoices with our gloves on. The only way to keep warm was to go and pack up books. There was a heater in the packing shed although it was a bit of a needle in a haystack.

After some toing and froing the builders eventually arrived. At the time Martin was in hospital. The first thing they did was to knock a hole in the office wall. I rang Pat who pointed out that they'd taken long enough to arrive and they might as well get on with it. The end result was a radiator in the office (luxury!) and a wood burner downstairs in the warehouse. This was supposed to be fed with wood, but occasionally Martin would gleefully fill it with damaged or otherwise unsaleable books - taking great pleasure in the fact that I couldn't bring myself to burn books, he would announce that if it was OK for the fascists to burn books then it was certainly OK for him!!

Books

An Old Gaffer's Tale was produced whilst I was at Merlin. It was a labour of love. Martin wrote and edited the book and read all the proofs. He was delighted to see his name in print on the front of a book and enjoyed the experience of visiting chandlers the length and breadth of the country in order to sell it.

Socialist Register

The *Register* was and still is an annual Merlin event. It would arrive from Ralph Miliband in manuscript form. Each contributor would have written their piece on different types of paper and in different formats. It was always exciting when it first arrived as the topics would have been under discussion for months and to see it in reality was always an event. Martin felt that the *Register* was important because it helped to identify Merlin as being firmly on the left and because it would also assist sales. We could sell the *Register* anywhere (and did) and usually some other titles on the back of it.

Edward Thompson

Martin and Edward were in almost daily contact. However, because his phone was bugged and Merlin's phone was also bugged, the phone never rang. It would shake and cough once and then we would know who was on the other end of the line.

Phone contact was made more interesting with the answerphone which contained the following message: 'Hello, this is a machine.' This informative missive would lure Edward into leaving bizarre announcements as to who was calling. He was Mrs Thatcher; he was Gorbachev, but never himself.

Miscellany

Martin taught me never to be rude to someone about their book. Remember it's their baby he would say. You would never tell anyone they had an ugly baby and so you must never tell an author they have a dreadful book.

To anyone who asked when he was retiring Martin would announce that he knew someone who had retired at 94 and lived to regret it.

Martin was full of stories - something that can be seen in *An Old Gaffer's Tale* - stories of cycling to school (a two day ride), stories of lying about his age to go to war and learning fast about life as a naval rating, stories about the war and the Normandy landings, stories about building the Partisan railway in Yugoslavia and stories of life in the Britain of the 50s and 60s.

He gave me a lot of space to try and come to terms with what I had just been through. He never pressurised me but stood back and listened. He put up with visits from *The Daily Mail* and break-ins from M15 and never once complained. When I think of Martin I first of all think of a smile and then of a cheery wave.

Sarah Tisdall
Publisher's assistant

Photocopy of letter to Sarah Tisdall

[handwritten: 3c/3]   *[handwritten: ← Censor's mark !!]*

[N PRESS LTD.
ROAD, LONDON, E.14
- 987 7959
ered No. 585114

                      to you to express my support for what you
had the courage to do and congratulate you on a public-spirited act.
I should also like to express my outrage that you have been s nt to
prison for revealing a political secret,not a military one - i.e. one
that has to be kept not from foreign governments but from the British
people.
           Under separate cover I am sending a copy of a book,
and also our catalogue. I shall be very glad to send any more books
that you might wish to read.
           By coincidence there will be a vacancy in our
small publishing house.After due consideration I am offering you
this job,should you wish to go into publishing. No doubt you will
want to know more about the job and have time to think about it;
the job will be held as long as is necessary.

           With every good wish,
               yours sincerely,

29 3 84   Martin Eve

DIRECTORS : MARTIN EVE, D. MUSSON, A. WEITZEL.

* * *

MERLIN'S LONG TERM ACCOUNTANT   MUNRO MOORE

I first met Martin over 40 years ago when he used to visit my parents. Tall, gangly, affable fellow with time to listen and encourage a lad only just in his teens to philosophise on a better world.

Many years later there would be great excitement in my own home as Martin was coming to visit. Many people wrapped up in the seriousness of everyday life lose that ability to communicate especially to the very young. My children always enjoyed talking with Martin.

Some people thought that Martin was a dreamer, always in a muddle, an absent-minded professor; not my Martin, he knew exactly where he was going and worked extremely hard to keep on course, and during the ups and downs always managed to see the humorous side.

While undergoing treatment he told me that he had just finished a course to reteach him how to get about (re-learning the simple things of life like taking a bus). NHS budgets being what they are, the course finished before he was taught how to get off the bus.

Martin a great friend.

Munro Moore
Accountant
                                        * * *

AT MALDEN ROAD   AGHDAS BIDHENDI

I consider myself a very lucky person. Fate brought me halfway across the world, from a small village in Iran to London, to meet and work for Martin. Someone once asked Martin if I was working for him. With his usual wit and consideration he replied: 'and not against me' - I was honoured.

My everlasting memory of Martin is a man of immense mental strength. He said one day he was organising boxes of books in his Isle of Dogs office and his then young son William said to him 'I always thought you had to be clever to be a publisher, but now I know that you only need to be strong.' When I came to the scene it was his immense strength of character that astonished me.

There is very little that I can say about his intelligence, wit and his devotion that anyone who ever had any contact with him did not notice. So, my tribute to him would only be sharing a few endearing memories.

I once entered the office excited about the birth of my first grandchild and said to Martin 'I feel extremely clever. I have just produced my first grandchild.' Without a pause and with a great smile he said 'I have seven!'

Lunch times were educational. He had made an unspoken rule about not talking business over lunch even when he was having a business lunch! Instead, you would be drawn into the most interesting conversation about past and present affairs. He was also a great listener. We were once talking about food and well-being. I, being the sceptic, was saying that when my children were young, I was doing my best to give them all the 'right food' and do all the 'right things'. But as it turned out they did not grow up to be particularly healthy, tall or beautiful (I was being modest!). Martin said 'and imagine if you had not!'

He never allowed his disability to get the better of him. One day he aimed to sit on a chair that had a mind of its own; I heard the disturbance in his office. I rushed to see what was happening, and Martin said, 'it's OK, I was having a fight with the chair and I just won.' The chair was knocked down in the middle of the room!

He loved and respected life. Just a few hours before his final farewell, he said that he had no fear of death because he had no experience of it! He also said that he was a very fortunate man as he was married to a brave and wonderful woman. And I knew for fact that it was indeed the great woman alongside the great man who had a lot to do with his happiness and love of life.

Aghdas Bidhendi
Accountant

* * *

REPPING FOR MARTIN   NATALIE JONES

I first met Martin when he was already ill but his openness about his illness ensured that it never seemed a problem except that he thought it better not to go the pub, and so I remember lovely lunches in the office with either Aghdas or Pat. It was at one of these lunches that he suggested taking my three young boys out on his boat and Martin must have read my face and said with his usual grin 'Don't worry, they would be quite safe with me'. My horror, however, was not about their safety but that anyone should want to take three London boys on a boat in the first place.

I admired his publishing and was proud to represent the Merlin and Seafarer lists and he was wonderful to work for because, as he used to say, 'having been a rep himself he could appreciate the difficulties'. As a result his commission cheque was always the first I received each month and I never took offence when he pointed out my omissions.

Martin's enthusiasm for life made it easier to comprehend something of the spirit in which he lived for the last few years of his life and faced his death. It was something to do with being alive until the last possible minute and knowing what is important to you and those around you regardless of what the outside world is talking about, and being able to make the most of being alive until we die. It was like that with Martin; he made you think about being alive.

I will never forget either Pat or Martin.

Gift (Ceslaw Milosz)
A day so happy.
Fog lifted early, I worked in the garden.
There was no thing on earth I wanted to possess.
I knew no one worth my envying him.
Whatever evil I had suffered, I forgot.
To think that once I was the same man did not embarrass me.
In my body I felt no pain
When straightening up, I saw blue sea and sails.

Natalie Jones
Publishers' representative
                              * * *

MERLIN AUTHORS

UNWAVERING ALLEGIANCE

GORDON LEFF

Martin was a person of courage and tenacity; he was also without self-display or opinionation. In over twenty years I never heard him mention his wartime exploits or any others. He combined deeply-held socialist convictions with sociability and a sense of humour (qualities not always found together) and his friends extended well beyond those who shared his beliefs. That was as true of his university days as of his subsequent life and publishing career.

At Cambridge, he made his political mark as the communist presence in the Union, the main university forum of debate. To do so in the late 1940s needed considerable nerve. The cold war had recently begun and threatened periodically to become a hot war through flashpoints like the Berlin blockade and airlift in 1948; the tensions were exacerbated by the various trials and persecutions in the communist countries, making the lot of a local communist, especially in a politically conscious society like Cambridge, a daunting one, and threatening future job prospects: something that Martin personally found after leaving the university as, because of adverse references, his first job was on a building site. Yet, in the Union, his calmly stated arguments and unstrident personality gained him a hearing, and friendly relations with political opponents. In consequence, he was probably the most influential, as well as least flamboyant, communist student of his day.

As a publisher, his successful creation of the Merlin Press in 1956, with its distinctive niche, and continuing to the present, speaks for itself. It again took nerve for him to leave a comparatively secure position with Michael Joseph to start on his own, without independent capital. Through a mixture of resourcefulness and imagination, however, he overcame lack of material resources. He supported his new books with reprints and translations, mainly of historical works, long out of print though still used as authorities, but also including some of Stendhal's novels not otherwise available. From the outset, though, he sought to publish new titles of a socialist or progressive nature, beginning with *Folksong-Plainsong* by George Chambers, which challenged the received view of the origins of plainsong. It carried a characteristically iconoclastic preface from R. Vaughan Williams attacking the blindness of 'bat-eyed musicologists'. It also created a new author in his mid-seventies.

The real impetus to new socialist works, however, came with the Soviet suppression of the Hungarian rising in late 1956 and the mass exodus from western communist parties which it precipitated. Those events, set in train the re-thinking of fundamental Marxist and socialist principles by the New Left. Among the most prominent revisionists was Edward Thompson, one of Martin's closest friends from Cambridge days, who undoubtedly influenced Martin. Martin became Thompson's principal publisher, also reprinting earlier works on *William Morris* and the *Making of the Working Class* in England. In addition to a succession of other new socialist works, translations and reprints, Martin from 1964 published the annual *Socialist Register* as a journal of socialist thought continuing to the present what the publications of the New Left had begun in the middle 1950s. In the very different conditions of post-1956, Merlin Press has thereby filled some of the place, albeit in a much more restricted way, of the Left Book Club before the Second World War. For a time, there was also a Merlin Book Club to make its publications more available.

Although Martin remained unwavering in his socialist allegiance, he was also open to more critical approaches to socialist theory, as in the two books which he encouraged me to write and which he published. He was as much editor as publisher, and carefully read an author's text, not to change its content, but to try to make it as clear and cogent - in his own words as 'dry' - as possible. I am sure that I was not alone in benefiting from his comments and queries made with characteristic economy.

The last twelve years of his life accentuated his qualities of commitment and staying power to which Merlin Press is his monument.

Gordon Leff
Fellow student Cambridge, comrade, author

* * *

FAREWELL SERVICE ADDRESS   ISTVÁN MÉSZÁROS

Martin and I became friends nearly forty years ago. We were taking part in a week-end conference, held in 'Beatrice Webb House,' which fused the two leading periodicals of the 'New Left' born in the aftermath of October/November 1956 - *Universities and Left Review* and *The New Reasoner* - into the short-lived first embodiment of a magazine called *New Left Review*. Sadly, in the four decades since that time many participants of that conference turned against their original commitment, moving in the opposite direction. That was not Martin's way. He always remained faithful to his socialist principles to which he had committed himself at the age of sixteen to seventeen, before volunteering for the Navy (and claiming to be older than he actually was, in order to make

that possible) at the outbreak of the war. As he told me, he had read
Marx's *Capital* when he was seventeen, and understood very little of it.
But it was more than enough, as he put it, to make him realise the
historical validity of the vision expressed in that work. Subsequently,
Martin's war experience and the solidarity and companionship of fellow
sailors - many of them from the most underprivileged working class
background - intensified his commitment; and the years of study at
Cambridge after being demobbed, shared with friends like Edward
Thompson, deepened his understanding of both the theoretical basis and
the broad practical dimensions of the social order which he wanted to see
emerge. In our last conversation, only a few days before he died, he told
me that he had had a very happy life and that he had found great
fulfilment and gratification in that he never had to reverse the course
chosen in his youth, that he never had to deviate from it. 'It was always
one line,' he said with calm serenity.

Martin was a unique publisher. His achievements over forty-two
years, with extremely limited financial resources, were and remain truly
without equal. How could he succeed in his enterprise, against all odds,
even under conditions of great adversity?

All those who knew him well can testify not only to the integrity and
coherence with which he pursued his publishing project, but also to his
determination and single-minded dedication to work. In order to secure
the conditions of independence - for publishing what he wanted in
accordance with his principles - he always conducted his business under
the most modest circumstances. And he did not hesitate to do everything,
from assessing and editing manuscripts to proof-reading, packing and
carting on his back the books in large sacks to the post office. I know how
hard Martin's daily routine was, because on occasions I helped him carry
the sacks filled with the daily order of books for mailing at the local post
office. Martin's unforgettable first publishing 'headquarters' were at
Fitzroy Square in London. They consisted of one room on the first floor,
size 8ft by 8, and a few shelves in the basement for storing the books to
be mailed. The room was furnished with two small desks and three
chairs: one for Martin, one for his secretary, and the third for people who
called at the office. We had to use a very large shoe-horn to be able to
squeeze into that small room. But the spirit that greeted us there was
great; well worth the squeezing. In complete contrast only as regards
space, Martin's second office, on the Isle of Dogs, offered equally modest
surroundings. Benefiting from a short lease, it occupied a huge
unheatable floor of a semi-derelict warehouse, later to be pulled down. In
this office Martin could store the total number of books published by The

Merlin Press. But in one little corner he had to install a prefabricated wooden hut, with a paraffin heater, so that he should not freeze to death. The second office on the Isle of Dogs, somewhat better in amenities, was still very modest, as was his third office, in North London, and the fourth and final one in Rendlesham. These were the material conditions of his enterprise, against the prevailing trend which seriously affected, and even bankrupted, several left-wing publishing houses. And over forty-two years he produced a list of lasting validity, envied by publishers of incomparably greater material resources. What Martin has achieved remains a great asset for the future which he believed in.

We loved Martin and we shall guard his memory. The best way to do it is to try to continue - in whatever way we can - the work to which he dedicated his life, in his spirit .

István Mészáros
Friend and author

* * *

ENDURING LEGACY   SHEILA ROWBOTHAM

I don't remember exactly when I first met Martin, but it was through Dorothy and Edward Thompson - probably in the 1960s. I do remember him telling me in the early days of the women's liberation groups about the position that Doris Lessing found herself in after the publication of *The Golden Notebook*.

In 1979 Lynne Segal, Hilary Wainwright and I produced 2,000 copies of *Beyond The Fragments* through friends at Islington Gutter Press. To our surprise - but also to our relief because it meant that we broke even, we sold the lot. Dave Musson, who was working for Martin at the time, was keen on Merlin publishing it and this brought me into more contact with Martin. It was also published then in the US, in Germany and in Brazil! The Germans re-issued it recently as a feminist classic and when I was in Brazil this year, I was told that a member of the Workers' Party had brought a copy back from exile in France, insisting that it be translated and that it had influenced them. A friend of mine who teaches English at the Sorbonne still uses it; however, the students are becoming increasingly bewildered by the political references.

When Martin published *Homeworkers' Worldwide* I was to experience his ingenious capacity to get books around the world again. I walked into the local bookshop in Santa Cruz to discover the only book they had in stock by me was *Homeworkers' Worldwide*.

'Not global,' protested Martin, who didn't hold with jargon, when we were trying to think of a title. However his political principles were impressive for in 1993, when the book was published, homeworkers were not exactly most publishers' idea of a best seller.

I had Repetitive Stress Injury badly in 1992-3 and could neither write nor type. So I dictated the little book onto audio tapes. I hated working like that, though the result was simple and clear so that Renana Jhabvala from the Self Employed Women's Association in India likes the book very much because she can use it in a practical way.

Of course I could not have found a more sympathetic publisher than Martin. Though he was in a much worse situation by then than I was, even at my worst, he was unfailingly kind. I can remember him taking me to a pub and us both going through complicated contortions to open doors and lift up our beer glasses.

Socialist Register brought me in touch with Martin again and he was as ever incredibly impressive in his attention to detail and his feeling for words. When he said he liked the article I wrote 'Dear Dr Marx,' I felt truly proud.

We talked on the phone again when I was organising the event on the *Communist Manifesto* in Conway Hall with Dave Timms and again Martin, by this time very ill, kept in touch and sent encouragement. He also put me in touch with James MacGibbon who was a link back to the 1947 commemoration which Martin remembered. But then they had been in the Royal Albert Hall; Marxism has rather come down in the world. Martin, however, believed in holding bridges, keeping paths open. He lived and worked against the odds. A postscript which he would appreciate is that Benjamin Cohen, an Israeli Marxist, wants to translate some pieces from *Socialist Register* into Hebrew. The Greek friend who sent me an e-mail added that the Israeli left is beleaguered at present. Martin's indefatigable tenacity has left us all a legacy which reaches out into some surprising places and will go on.

Sheila Rowbotham
Author
                                        * * *

THE GOOD PUBLISHER   FRANCIS BECKETT

I first met Martin Eve right at the start of the eighties. I ran the publicity department of the National Union of Agricultural and Allied Workers, and wanted to see Reg Groves' classic history of rural trade unionism, *Sharpen the Sickle*, re-published. I was told that Martin was the publisher who would take it on with the perfect mixture of enthusiasm and professionalism.

He did. By the time I met him, he had read the book from cover to cover, and recognised clearly that this was no ordinary trade union history. He saw - as the NUAAW general secretary Jack Boddy wrote in the introduction to the Merlin edition - that 'it's not a dull catalogue of people and places, spiced with uncritical eulogies of presidents and general secretaries. It is the history of the awakening of the exploited rural poor.'

I have the book Martin published in 1981 in front of me as I write. I remember the thought and understanding that went into commissioning the simple but very effective line drawing on the cover, the pleasure and pride that he put into a book which was never going to make anyone rich, but which he was sure mattered.

Years later, in the 1990s, working on a history of Britain's communists, *Enemy Within*, which had been commissioned by John Murray, I came across several marvellous manuscripts, most of which will probably never be published, but which, if this were a society which valued its roots, would be fought over by publishers.

The best of them all was a wonderfully written account of the misery and bafflement of Communists in 1956, written from the vantage point of the *Daily Worker* newsroom by Alison McLeod. It contained stories never before published, and I knew it deserved a wider audience. But in today's publishing climate, I despaired of her ever finding one.

I reckoned without Martin. *The Death of Uncle Joe* was published by Merlin Press in 1997, with Martin's usual enthusiasm and care.

Shortly before his death, Martin published a book by me - the paperback of *Enemy Within*. I could tell that he was very ill, but that did not seem to diminish at all either his enthusiasm or his professionalism.

He was everything that a good publisher was supposed to be before the conglomerates moved in and vandalised the industry: thoughtful, sensitive, encouraging, patient, discriminating, with useful things to say about everything one wrote, and always able to sound as though any book was as big a part of his life as it was of the author's.

Francis Beckett
Author

* * *

AN IMPORTANT FIGURE   ADRIAN HOGBEN

My wife and I consider ourselves fortunate to have known Martin Eve, although it was only in the last year of his life.

During that year we worked with him in producing our edited posthumous autobiography of my father Lancelot Hogben, which Martin had bravely agreed to publish. He was a kind and generous man, whom we came to respect and admire.

The publishing world has lost an important figure at a time when the ranks of independent publishers are diminishing.

Adrian Hogben
Author
                              * * *

SEAFARER AUTHORS

Seafarer Books was started thirty-one years ago, as an imprint of Merlin Press, with the publication of *In Grandma's Wake* by the late Frank Mulville, a friend and author over many years. It was at Frank's suggestion that Martin added Seafarer Books to his list, which reflected his abiding interest in the sea.

CLOSE ENCOUNTERS   ANTHONY BAILEY

The first time I encountered Martin was afloat, on the Blackwater, in an Old Gaffers' Race in light airs. My wife and I in our small gaff cutter had just been favoured by a miraculous private breeze and had overtaken twenty boats. But as we came up to the promontory called the Stone, the opposition caught us up. We tacked across the river. 'Does that boat realize we're on starboard?' I asked Margot. It didn't seem to. At the last minute I yelled for right-of-way and the somewhat undercanvassed-looking smack yacht in our path came gently about. 'Privateer,' it said on the stern. The helmsman appeared to be deep in conversation with his crew about something else altogether. But when we next crossed tacks Privateer was ahead, and remained so to the finish.

Thereafter I met Martin in his ground-floor, shop-front office in Malden Road, Chalk Farm, sandwiched between an Afro hairdresser's and a mini-cab firm. I had gone to introduce myself and discuss a book of mine, a piece of sailing autobiography, he was planning to bring out. Knowing nothing of his publishing ventures, I was intrigued to see some of the Merlin Press as well as Seafarer backlist on his shelves: Socialist Register; E.P. Thompson's William Morris; Frank Mulville... My other publishers at that moment held sway in lofty modern office blocks in Chelsea and Manhattan, somewhat welcoming in Chelsea, somewhat haughty and remote in Manhattan. Malden Road was refreshing. Martin and I sat with mugs of coffee. I couldn't help but notice how he lifted his mug pressed between his two fists, fingers knotted together. If he was crippled by illness, its severity was determinedly camouflaged.

Martin published that and another sea - or coastfaring book of mine, but he had only a few years of sailing and publishing to come. I met him at anniversaries - Privateer's thirtieth in his hands, held at Tollesbury; Seafarer's thirtieth, at Pin Mill - and though he was increasingly frail, he was courageously charming. I wish I had known him longer. Should we meet in a sailors' heaven, I shall - whatever tack he is on - concede the right of way.

Anthony Bailey
Author
                              * * *

SCHOOLFELLOWS' MEETING HENRY SWAIN

The letter said, 'Sorry I kept your manuscript so long, but would you come and see me?' There was a Merlin Press letterhead and it was signed Martin Eve. Was this the break for a first time author?

I inquired about this firm that I had rather randomly selected from a list of publishers in the *Writer's Handbook*.

'Distinguished, highly respected left wing.' I was told by my bookseller friends, 'academically OK and usually reviewed in the papers and magazines'. Then they added an afterthought, 'Oh, yes, they publish books about the sea'.

My book was about the sea.

I didn't know what I expected a publisher's office to look like, but I had not anticipated a room made of books. Shelves along the walls were overflowing with old and new works by famous authors: some were by or about my socialist heroes - William Morris, E.P. Thompson, Georg Lukács. For someone who liked books this was an Aladdin's cave. There was just one man in a sort of cleared space in the middle of it all. Relaxed and welcoming. The sound of typewriting came from behind a heap of papers and boxes, but otherwise the Merlin Press was just Martin Eve.

I found space to sit down by removing some newly printed volumes from a chair and we talked about my manuscript. It was a story of the Royal Navy in the Second World War and about a recent voyage to north Russia in my own yacht. Amazingly my prospective publisher knew even more than I did about the war at sea and sailing yachts.

Suddenly he looked at me, 'I think we've met before'. A blink of time, and there was a thirteen-year-old schoolboy called Eve at Bryanston in 1937. We had shared the same world of war, sailing and socialism, but for sixty odd years our paths had never crossed.

I was, I reminded myself, talking to the director of a successful business. We discussed what was the possible readership among yachtsmen or Royal Navy people, was there an American interest? The phone kept ringing, and at such moments I had time to gaze around. Gradually the identity of the piled high room came to me. It wasn't an office at all - it was a military headquarters - not of a regular battalion but of a partisan unit. It transmitted its orders in the form of books and magazines to invisible soldiers fighting for a different kind of future.

That was my first meeting with him about the book, the first of many others.

Then came the last time and I didn't know it was the last time. The occasion was a party at the Butt and Oyster at Pin Mill. There were well known writers present - more heroes. Martin made one of his interesting and endearing speeches to welcome his guests. The clarity and sense of his words belied the frailty of his body. Not for a moment, though, did I feel sorry for him: he wasn't somebody you felt sorry for.

In retrospect it seemed to be the only sunny day in a rainy cold summer. I see him still sitting on a table to speak. Behind him through the window there is the blue river Orwell and beyond it the low shore of the Suffolk he loved so well.

It was time to go and I have another memory of him. He was being helped by his wife, Pat, into his wheelchair. She did it with a kind of reverence. I felt privileged to see such warmth and gentle affection.

Some of us have principles that get set aside. Martin lived by principle all the time; I don't grieve for him; he has become another of my heroes.

Henry Swain
Author with many shared life experiences

* * *

A VERY CIVILISED FRIEND   RAYNER UNWIN

I ought to have known Martin when I was a publisher: we had been contemporaries and both had lists that tended to be left of centre. But it was not until my firm had been swallowed up, and I tried my hand at authorship instead, that I actually met him. He had kept to a sensible small size, and wasn't much interested in trade politics. I chose him because of his Seafarer Books imprint. I had written a book of maritime history that was distinctly 'middle ground'. This had been a complimentary term a decade or two previously, but to the new conglomerates it was anathema. Martin didn't mind. He was much more concerned that I had muddled up two technical navigational terms - variation and deviation. He sorted me out as a good editor should. That was his strength - he could do everything himself. Nowadays editors and book production are far less influential than finance and marketing. With Martin it was the reverse, and it was refreshing to call on his Chalk Farm office (lodged as far as I remember between a barber and a greengrocer) and receive his undivided attention. The room was splendidly untidy, but a chair could always be unearthed, and his hard-working girl-Friday would retire to the back room to make tea. Our talk was never departmentalised. It ranged over every aspect of the books he was dealing with - mine and others. I saw from his list that he had revived the popular science books of Lancelot Hogben, which had been our firm's first bestsellers in the 1930s, and I hoped that they might repeat the magic for him. But I suspect it was the merit of the contents rather than the sales potential that had attracted him. He liked choosing and producing books of consequence, and the process of actually selling them seemed less interesting. It was also becoming increasingly impersonal for any publisher of his size.

Our talk quite quickly dealt with the immediate problems relating to my book. Although he took no part in it Martin was always interested in hearing what was going on in the book trade, and for the most part we agreed in deploring it. After that we would be all at sea. That was where Martin's love lay, and he always seemed completely happy at the prospect of messing around in boats. I'm not a sailor myself so I never saw him in action, but I was a good listener to his stories and marvel still at his determination, despite crippling disability, to sail at every possible opportunity, and to relish every moment of it. Books and boats made him a very civilised friend.

Rayner Unwin
Fellow publisher and author

* * *

SEAFARING DAYS

MARTIN EVE - A REAL 'OLD GAFFER' JON WAINWRIGHT

It is a moot point whether the now accepted nautical term 'Old Gaffer' refers to an anachronistic gaff-rigged vessel, or to the said vessel's skipper. It is also a moot point whether the term is derogatory in terms of being considered out-dated, or whether it is cocking a snoot at convention with piratical individualism. I prefer the latter!

The confusion between 'old gaffer' the boat and 'old gaffer' the person is largely due to the fact that the boat often reflects the person - or is it the other way round. Did Martin choose *Privateer*, or did *Privateer* choose Martin? His book *An Old Gaffer's Tale* gives no real clues. She was in a fairly forlorn state when he first saw her. He talks about '*a lot of rigging all over the place and a long bowsprit pointed ahead*' and then most illogically ... '*I knew this was the boat I wanted*'. He then makes excuses about her being '*a fine boat for cruising*' ... '*no possibility that we would outgrow Privateer*' ... '*We should not begrudge the labour*' ... No doubt in my mind that *Privateer*, the 1930 creation of Gostelow of Boston, a real character in himself, sought out Martin as a kindred spirit. Martin was thus correct to surmise '*she would prove to be a rewarding boat*'.

It was no surprise that the pair of them ended up in the Tollesbury of the 60s, rather than Burnham, Brightlingsea, West Mersea or even Maldon. Frost & Drake's yard had changed little since the sailing smack days, and back then they still did much repair work to 'real' boats like *Privateer*. Unlike many fishing villages which can be very insular, Tollesbury's links with Victorian and Edwardian professional yachting gave rise to a very special kind of 'local,' who had often seen more of life than the city visitor. America's Cup Racing had been in the blood, and some pretty important people could be seen in Tollesbury - I remember one local rightly boasting that he had three cabinet ministers meeting in his front parlour. The Crab and Winkle Railway, the pier and the mad plans were all part of the eccentricity of the place which was Martin, *Privateer* and Tollesbury.

Martin and *Privateer*'s exploits were real 'Old Gaffering,': often in complete contrast to the modern pundit's view of how one should go sailing. Compared with today's plastic yachts with all the gizmos such as satellite navigation, Autohelm, radar, wind speed indicators etc.., it was a real tribute to Martin's skills and courage that they reached safely all their destinations - although he always took the precaution of saying that he was going 'towards' somewhere rather than 'to' somewhere. In-mast furling and roller reefing headsails on luffspars aided by 3-speed self-tailing winches of today's yachts contrasted with the heavy spars, flax sails and 'Armstrong's Patent' on *Privateer*, yet many a sea mile between the Baltic and Brittany the pair put under them, while the pundit's plastic yachts lay lifeless in marinas.

It is not to say that Martin was a narrow-minded traditionalist. He spoke very kindly of the Seafarer echo sounder and the Sea Fix Radio Direction finder, and they were quite advanced 'gizmo's' in the 60s and 70s. The square plastic Sportyak dinghy, which Martin conceded 'No one could say was easy on the eye' (but would carry 6 adults!) was a principal means of identifying *Privateer* from the many other gaffers sporting ex-Admiralty grey paint and tan sails. Martin sailed *Privateer* in the way he did because he got the most out of it. Entering strange harbours under sail, towing up the Kiel canal, or bow-hauling along a dyke, or kedging with an anchor were all part of the repertoire.

We still have old gaffers or smack races and classic boat festivals - many more than 20 years ago. Many traditional boats have been lovingly restored or rebuilt even better than new. It is part of a fashionable cult to sail a smack or classic yacht. But rarely do we see the type of partnership that Martin and *Privateer* enjoyed, which can only be engendered by experiences shared by special personalities, both human and boat.

I am honoured to have known such a person on such a boat, whether it was at Tollesbury on a nearby mooring, a secluded anchorage on an East Coast River, or at a Rally. I am privileged to have known a real old gaffer.

Jon Wainwright
Old Gaffers Association

* * *

PRIVATEER ROMANCES   GILL JACOBS

I first met Martin soon after I left university. A friend started to work for Merlin Press in Fitzroy Square, and through her, because I had sailed before, I was invited for a weekend aboard *Privateer*. This was my first experience of sailing anything other than small boats. And what a wonderful introduction it was! Martin revelled in showing newcomers the ropes, and inducting them into the '*Privateer* experience' - the lack of acquaintance with the engine (rarely used), the rationing of tooth cleaning water, the intricacies of lighting Tilley lamps and the hissing sound when successfully alight, the knack of using plumb lines in shallow water with

dense fog and a broken echo sounder (without letting go), the art of
peeing over the side of the boat, the pleasure of collecting sea spinach,
the terror of keeping watch in the middle of the night while others slept,
in the eye of a storm, anchored in the middle of shipping lanes in the
Thames estuary, the eeriness of passing huge buoys with clanging bells in
the English Channel in the dark. And last but not least, the accounts of
Martin entertaining customs officers on re-entering British waters, with
swigs of Kumel from the ship's supplies!

What I remember most about those early days' sailing, was Martin's
tremendous capacity for friendship. Despite the age gap between us he
did not talk down, or keep a distance. He loved to share his good fortune
in owning *Privateer*, and did so with such an infectious sense of fun and
enthusiasm. Always you were aware of Martin's total oneness with the
boat. You knew you were in safe hands. His piercing eyes, on the look-
out for a change in the wind, gave him an alertness that was never
diminished by his engaging conversation. He may have distracted the
listener from noticing the elements, but he was always in total control.

There must be something really special about *Privateer*, because I was
present on that fateful charter trip when Martin first met Pat, and later, it
was on a sailing weekend with Martin that I first met my husband.

What a privilege, at the funeral, to be in the company of so many
people equally affected by Martin's unique combination of intellectual
engagement, political commitment, practical competence and deep
humanity. He had a wonderful capacity to fully engage with whoever he
was with - his direct gaze, his twinkling eyes, and his humorous, knowing
smile. Hearing from others of his bravery in the last years of his illness
only adds to the picture of a man who was able to face up to difficulties,
and still find ways of living life to the full.

Gill Jacobs
Crew

* * *

CHANCE ENCOUNTER   JOHN MAXWELL

On Saturday, 5 May 1984 at 20:00 hours I entered Holehaven in my
gaff cutter *Fiat Lex* and passed *Privateer* and anchored. I was bound for
the Swale. On Sunday at 06:30 having got the forecast NE5/6 I took in 2
reefs and prepared to sail. *Privateer* had already left Holehaven bound for
Tollesbury. When we were almost ready to weigh anchor *Privateer*
returned and anchored and Martin shouted across that it was rough

outside. Shortly thereafter Martin and Pat rowed across and came aboard and invited me and my crew Clive for coffee. We decided there was no question of going North of Sheppey to the East Swale and that we would go to Queenborough and that as long as we got to the mouth of the Medway before LW we could drink coffee on *Privateer*. So we rowed across and boarded *Privateer* and Pat made coffee. I told her that in all my sailing I had never before had real coffee. Martin said he had watched us come into Holehaven the night before and admired our high peaked rig. As we departed, Pat pressed a packet of ground coffee into my hand. Just as we were hauling up the anchor Martin came rowing across with my hat which I had left behind.

We sailed out of Holehaven and reached Queenborough without mishap. We met up with some friends and invited them aboard for real coffee. We had no coffee pot or filter but used a handkerchief to filter the coffee. The next day we returned to our mooring in the Gravesend basin and saw that *Privateer* was alongside the wall.

After that event 14 years ago I never again saw *Privateer* or Martin or Pat. I saw the review of the *An Old Gaffer's Tale* which I bought and enjoyed.

I heard nothing more until I read with sadness in the Old Gaffers Log of Martin's death.

It is odd to think that my path and Martin's path only crossed for less than an hour and that that hour sticks in my mind as a curiously vivid memory.

John Maxwell
Fellow sailor

* * *

FRIENDS

A TRUE FRIEND   DR MICHAEL HATHORN

I first met Martin Eve about 1972 at a friend's house in Savernake Road, and was most interested to learn that he was the publisher of *Socialist Register*, which I had been reading since its launch in 1964. But it was to be another 8 years before I met him again, when I joined the local Labour Party branch of which he was Chair at the time.

Martin was interested in everyone he met. He soon found out the limitations and the positive attributes of his many friends. He made allowances for their limitations and had the ability to draw out and amplify the positive sides of their personalities. He seldom argued with his friends: during discussions he would often deal with a thorny issue by asking the right question and thus taking the argument further towards its conclusion.

When Martin learned in 1981 that I was an occasional dinghy sailor, he immediately invited me to join him and Pat on the first of perhaps a dozen voyages I have made with them and other sailing companions on *Privateer*. It is necessary for the skipper of a vessel to enjoy the trust of his or her crew, and in the final analysis this trust has to be earned. The skipper must be able to take the right decision in an emergency, and at the same time be able to plan the next stage of the voyage with due regard to the weather forecast, the peculiarities of the tides in different coastal seas, together with that premonition of possible dangers that comes to some from learning from a lifetime of sailing.

In 1983 Martin and Gary made one of the passages in *Privateer* across the North Sea. They sailed from Harwich to Holland, through the Kiel Canal into the Baltic, and back through the Lim Fjord which bisects Jutland. They were joined at various stages by Pat and others of his family. Martin invited me to join him and Gary for the return passage from Jutland to Harwich. It was my first journey across the open sea. We were out of sight of land for five days, and with the battery in the radio compass failing, we were able to get only a few directions from the transmissions of the Texel Light Ship. But with accurate dead reckoning from compass and log, and calculations of the tides, Martin plotted our course home. Towards the end of the afternoon of the sixth day, Martin laconically announced that Harwich should be appearing over the horizon within the next 20 minutes. Sure enough, 15 minutes later there it was, dead ahead. That was a high point in my trust in Martin as a skipper as well as a friend.

With the onset of his illness and its effect particularly on his hands and feet, Martin continued sailing in *Privateer*. On one of these trips when we tied up in Shoreham on the South Coast, Martin wanted to phone Pat to tell her of our safe arrival. But at low tide, he was faced with a climb with his weakened hands and feet up an 18-foot vertical iron ladder. Gary and I solved the problem by slinging a bowline under Martin's arms and belaying the rope round a capstan on the dock while he slowly went up the ladder to make his phone call, and then return.

In 1988 I was privileged to be invited yet again to sail in *Privateer*. The leg of the journey southwards from Dieppe was to terminate in Fécamp. With a strong northerly wind blowing, and the tide racing across the narrow entrance to Fécamp, the approach was tricky. Martin made his judgement, and wedged in the stern with his back against the tiller, he guided *Privateer* as straight as an arrow under full sail into the narrow entrance. That was courage in the face of adversity, added to his ever present skill.

With his increasing disability, Martin never complained. He was determined to continue living his life to the full, to the best of his abilities. Until he and Pat moved from London to Suffolk, my annual copy of *Socialist Register* was delivered in person by Martin; the last time it took him a full 20 minutes to make the short journey down the street on his crutches.

Martin will be remembered by friends from the many facets of his life: social, nautical, literary, political and personal. All will bear testimony to a true friend, trusted and with great courage.

Michael Hathorn
Friend and political activist

* * *

AGROUND!   MARY HOSEASON

Some moments spent in Martin's company. They show a fun loving personality, steely will and a spontaneous and demonstrative nature that complemented his awesome intellect.

Leisure?

I remember a clear sunny day, driving to the east coast for a day visit to *Privateer*. We set off for a short sail. Past the hulk of Bradwell power station, with a light breeze blowing. Views of the open sea sparkling away towards the horizon, whilst we went about. Suddenly all became urgent; rapid instructions to crew, including clueless me. We were heading towards some elusive sailing channel, but I fear not enough sea, as we ground gracefully upright on a mud bank. We had eight to nine hours to enjoy the view, wild life and one another.

The sun shone, the waders waded and after excellent grub from talented galley hand, Martin cheerfully lead 'team cleaning' of the hull, as the perfect opportunity had presented itself. The novice passed on this task.

Light fading, birds roosting, more sustenance and we sat with a ration of rum, as the inky darkness arrived with the lapping of the returning tide. Several hours of 'lapping' are required before a *bona fide*, wooden, gaff rigged Boston fishing smack gets anywhere near 'floating'. It is nine-ish and engine on? No way - Martin in over the side and it's the dinghy. Having built it oneself, it's the thing to do. He is rowing up the Blackwater towing four tons of ballast and I am not talking about the crew. Pat was glued to the bow with torch looking for and finding the mooring buoy - brilliant. All aboard the dinghy and we row off to shore.

Ten thirty-ish and Martin is driving sedately in the Wartburg, through quiet dark Sunday night Essex countryside. The ultimate in modern galley slave has passed round cups of coffee, which we slurp 'on the wheel' so to speak. Suddenly I hear Martin remarking in his low, very considered tone, that he thought Mary had been very stoic, considering she had never actually expressed any wish to go sailing.

Domesticity

Martin was a covert parkin eater. Hearing from Pat that he would be self-catering for a few days, whilst she was away improving her mind, he immediately intimated he could cope and that he would make a parkin, which he loved to do. This was not entirely favourably received. He then remarked *sotto voce* to me, that his plan would succeed. He would need to keep it for some days, to mature, and that it would be hidden in a wardrobe, and all the better for it too.

A Cherished Moment
On returning one late autumn afternoon to tea at 62B, the sitting room had been refurbished. When Martin put on a lamp, I remarked on a lovely small sampler, worked in yellow thread, and which was framed and had been hung above his arm chair. He flew across the room and kissed my cheek; he was just so pleased (he had completed this as a boy).

Martin's glass was always half full; never half empty. His optimism and sense of humour shone through all adversity.

Mary Hoseason
Friend

* * *

MARTIN 'A DEAR FRIEND'   JOHN MAHON

I first met Martin when I was invited to lunch by his wife Pat.
It was a beautiful summer's day in July 1987. Pat took me out to the garden where we found him, sitting on a small metal and canvas stool; it became apparent that he had strategically placed the stool in such a way in order to gain the best possible purchase on the four pronged fork which he was working through the dry soil with a purpose. He stopped his work to welcome me not just with warm words but also with the most wonderful smile that I could only compare to that of one other very special person in my life up to that day. From that day onwards, Martin was to become another very special person in my life; we became very close friends and I frequently visited Pat and Martin's home. Pat's culinary delights certainly were something to look forward to, but the things that Martin and I got up to in the garden and the huge garage were the big attraction for me. He would plan projects that we could work on such as the 'over the side' wooden ladder he wanted to make for *Privateer*. He designed the ladder and had every little detail so precise that even I could put it together with his patient coaching. Before I met Martin, the nearest I came to D.I.Y. was seeing the products in the suppliers' shop window and the ads on their vans; so it was a great thrill to discover that I could actually do such things...

One of our proudest achievements was a polished seat for the 'heads' in *Privateer*. I believe that Martin could always get the best out of anyone; he most certainly did with me.

As the years went by our friendship became stronger and stronger. I once asked if he would read something I had written and despite the fact that it had become extremely difficult for him to hold a pen, much less write with one, he actually wrote down his comments by HAND and not just a brief note, but a long detailed letter... No easy options for Martin... Oh no! That was not his way!

I sat by his bedside thirty hours before he left us, and I know he knew it was me sitting there; he gave me that 'special smile' for the last time.

And that will always be with me.

John Mahon
Friend

* * *

DRAWING THE THREADS TOGETHER

WALTER'S TRIBUTE AT MARTIN'S FAREWELL

I have had the good luck to be Martin's brother-in-law for more than fifty years.

Martin wanted his funeral to be not a time of mourning but a celebration of a life for which he was grateful - a life which we may see as purposeful, kindly and, in the end, heroic. He was an idealist, and one for whom ideals were the springboards of action. His life enriched others in various unostentatious ways.

He was still at school, at Bryanston, when the second world war broke out. To serve his country in a struggle against Nazi and Fascist aggression and oppression, he successfully pretended to be older than he was so that he could join the Royal Navy as soon as possible. In the corvette *Samphire* and the destroyer *Talybont* he served in dangerous waters, and was wounded in eye and neck.

As a Cambridge undergraduate he joined expeditions to help Balkan countries which had suffered through the war. He worked first on the building of a railway in Jugoslavia and next on the building of a dam in Bulgaria. He won the title of shock worker for outstanding effort.

Later, through many years of publishing as Merlin Press, working miracles on a shoestring, he served mankind by making more widely known those aspects of modern thought which he deemed would improve the world: thought such as is embodied in the writing of his great friend the late Edward Thompson. It was significant that one of the early Merlin publications was Thompson's book on William Morris: for Martin was a socialist-humanist in the tradition of Morris. For him Socialism was nothing if not an instrument for the betterment of humankind.

A lasting belief in the core of his early ideals and the conviction that what he was doing was worthwhile kept him going through years of crippling illness; years in which he benefited from Pat's expert and unstinting care. Only two weeks before his death he was completing the latest edition of *Socialist Register*, which he had nursed through many editions.

Martin inherited from his father a love of sailing and the sea, and from his mother a love of music, which showed itself in a remarkably early talent as a pianist and organist and in enjoyment of his part as a boy chorister in the great singing of Winchester Cathedral.

He shared with others his love of sailing, through voyages on the sturdy *Privateer*, through his writing about them and through the publication of Seafarer Books, which included the works of the late Frank Mulville; one of the finest modern yachtsmen-writers of the sea.

Gradually the loss of the use of hands and feet robbed Martin of much that in sailing and music had given him pleasure, but he never complained or indulged in self-pity.

Instead he counted the good things in his life: Pat's care and companionship; happy memories of boyhood with his sister at Orford, of Cambridge days and of family life with Betty at Bristol and Redbourne; his lasting friendships; his conviction of the worth of his work; the knowledge that his children were making good use of their lives; and the sight of his seven happily developing grandchildren, from young Tom at the threshold of school up to Laurie, thriving on marine studies at university, the valuable crewman of Martin's last voyages.

Martin would have been the last man to claim it, but to me he was a man cast in a quietly heroic mould.

Walter Kemsley
Brother in Law

* * *

A DOCTOR'S FAREWELL DR JOHN SCADDING

Martin was my patient and friend for some 12 years. It is an honour for me to pay a personal tribute to him. We met when Martin was experiencing the first symptoms of an illness that was to become a seriously disabling neuropathy. Throughout a lengthy period of diagnosis Martin was stoical and endlessly tolerant of the investigations. The news that his neuropathy was related to underlying malignant disease was received by Martin with equanimity and followed by relevant and searching questions about the effects of his illness, possible treatments and prognosis. With Martin's enthusiastic participation, several treatments were tried. Some made him feel rotten and frankly did him no good. Martin never complained. Eventually, long term treatment was established.

During this time I got to know Martin well. We found that there were things we shared - a love of sailing and a fascination with tales of exploration and human endurance. I came to understand Martin's deeply held moral values and political views and his ability to discuss these with great clarity and persuasion. His belief in the power of the written word and his love of books were obvious. We had similar views about social issues and in particular health care and the NHS. I greatly respected Martin's honesty and integrity and his guiding socialist principles. However serious the subject, Martin was never intense. He had immense charm and an infectious love of life and sense of humour.

I began to look forward to Martin's out-patient visits to the hospital. As his disability increased, the expertise began to flow in both directions. Ever practical, Martin had ingenious ideas to improve all sorts of things, for example, the splints to correct his footdrop, or the grips on his elbow crutches. I quickly learnt that for Martin such equipment needed to be tough. It had to stand up to the demands of an active life which Martin refused to give up, including the running of the Merlin Press and, of course, off-shore sailing aboard *Privateer*. My first weekend aboard *Privateer* with Martin and Pat was an eye opener for me. Martin never denied his disability, he just coped with it and got on with things with great patience, never showing signs of frustration and always with that characteristic cheerful demeanour. That first sailing weekend was truly inspirational for me.

My initial misgivings about developing a personal friendship with Martin and Pat, whilst continuing in the role of being Martin's neurologist, proved unnecessary and groundless. For Martin there was never a problem about this. I was simply embraced by Pat and Martin's friendship, their kindness and their generosity.

In 1986 Martin sent me a copy of his book *An Old Gaffer's Tale* inscribed 'In appreciation for keeping me afloat'. I felt then, and do now, that my role in keeping Martin afloat was minimal. The person who did, of course, was Pat, whose utterly devoted care for, and care of Martin became another gold standard for me.

For most people as disabled as Martin became, the development of new symptoms found to be due to bowel cancer, already with spread to the liver, would have been enough for them to throw in the towel. Martin simply took it in his stride. He quietly got on with yet more chemotherapy following surgery, while continuing to meet publishing deadlines, often involving frenetic activity. During this time Martin took delivery of the Velocipede and he wrote to me about this just a few months ago. I will quote from this letter and will leave you with Martin's words. For me these typify his optimism in the face of adversity and his indomitable and courageous spirit. We shall sorely miss him. I quote: 'You cannot imagine what it is like to spring from years of disability into this sudden comfortable and reasonably fast mobility. Currently, I am riding it around the huge car park here, but have made the journey from home and back (over a mile) and am in training for more ambitious journeys'.

John Scadding
Friend and neurologist

* * *

OBITUARIES

THE GUARDIAN   4 NOVEMBER 1998

In 1956 Martin Eve, who has died of cancer aged 74, founded the small, socialist publishing house, Merlin Press. Eight years later came the first edition of the annual *Socialist Register*; just three weeks ago he was working on proofs of the next edition. In the years in between, Martin was to publish such authors as István Mészáros, Georg Lukács and Ernest Mandel. In the 1970s there were several of Sheila Rowbotham's early works, and collections of Edward (E P) Thompson's essays, including the brilliant *Writing By Candlelight* and *The Poverty Of Theory*.

Through careful husbandry Martin was able to respond to the radical wave which began in the late 1950s. His first successes came in 1958 with two translations of Stendhal, after which he moved quickly into the then profitable area of reprints. By the middle 1960s he had a notable list of classic history texts, including books by Helen Cam, Jane Harrison, H.L. Gray, Maurice Powicke and Louis Berens.

It was, however, his political publishing that was to be at the centre of his activities, with new books, translations and reprints. There was a reprint of Ralph Miliband's *Parliamentary Socialism* and Thompson's revised *William Morris*. There was a four-volume facsimile reprint of *The Poor Man's Guardian*, introduced by Patricia Hollers, and Harney's *The Red Republican* and *The Friend Of The People*.

Martin was born and brought up in Orford on the Suffolk coast. His father, a well-known yachtsman, had retired there to oversee the Butley Oysterage. His mother, a Labour councillor for many years, was especially involved in child welfare issues. Martin won scholarships to Winchester Cathedral Choir School - music remained one of the joys of his life - and Bryanston, which he entered at the age of 13.

Already influenced by his mother's socialist ideas, in his late teens he moved towards communism. When Nazi Germany invaded the Soviet Union in 1941 Martin demonstrated his practical support for the anti-fascist cause by falsifying his age and joining the Royal Navy. As an ordinary seaman he took part in the 1942 Algiers landing, and was a junior officer on a destroyer during the 1944 Normandy invasion.

After being demobilised in 1946 he read history at Cambridge. There he met E P Thompson and, like many of his student generation, went to work on the Yugoslav railway project in the summer of 1947, as did both Edward and Dorothy Thompson. They and Martin were to remain close friends.

Thompson was also a great influence on Martin, who tried to follow the historian into the academic world of adult education. There may have been additional reasons but Martin's politics certainly proved, as for others, an obstacle that in the late 1940s and early 1950s was too great a barrier. So the first half of the 1950s found him working as a representative for the publishers, Michael Joseph; then came Merlin Press. His capital was always limited, and in the early years each book had to pay for the one that followed.

His father had encouraged both Martin and his sister, at a remarkably early age, to familiarise themselves with the intricacies of sailing; as indeed Martin was to do with his own children. In 1965 he bought *Privateer* - a converted fishing smack - and 20 years on he wrote *An Old Gaffer's Tale*, a lively account of his sailings along the East coast, across the English Channel and into the Baltic. It became one of a new Merlin series and Seafarer Books became a flourishing niche of narrative writings on sailing - to which several distinguished sailing writers contributed.

Martin's life changed radically in 1986, when he was diagnosed with lymphoma, and for the remaining 12 years of his life he became steadily more incapacitated. He walked with crutches in the final decade, until his last year, when he could only move by crutches or wheelchair.

But the work of Merlin Press continued. He was greatly helped, financially, in these last years by one friend in particular, but no help would have been sufficient had Martin not showed a quite extraordinary tenacity of purpose and toughness of character and spirit. The role of his second wife, Pat, was central; and her caring devotion did not falter or diminish.

Martin Eve was always helpful to those who worked in the publishing world. He had a wide circle of friends in both European and American publishing. He leaves his books, his music - and his sailing. He is survived by one daughter, two sons and their mother, and his wife Pat. He left many friends.

John Saville
Founding editor of *Socialist Register*

* * *

THE INDEPENDENT   11 NOVEMBER 1998

Martin Eve was a remarkable figure in post-war British publishing. He founded the Merlin Press in 1956 when he published G.B. Chambers's *Folksong-Plainsong* on the origins of English folksong, and worked continuously for Merlin until the week of his death.

Eve is probably best known for the books he published by the historian E.P. Thompson. Eve and Thompson enjoyed a lifelong friendship, which began at Cambridge, where Eve, an alumnus of Winchester Cathedral Choir School and the then progressive Bryanston, read History at Corpus Christi College. They had both served in the Second World War (Thompson in the Army in Italy, Eve in the Navy - he was present at D-Day), and they returned to undergraduate studies filled with inspiration from their wartime experience. They were young men committed to building a better future, and like many of their generation they joined the Communist Party.

With Thompson and others Eve participated enthusiastically in volunteer brigades working to rebuild Yugoslavia and Bulgaria. This led to an enduring interest in the Balkans and perhaps somehow shaped him as a 'partisan' - a word of defiance, comradeship and commitment that summed up so much of what he did.

After Cambridge, Thompson joined the extra-mural department at Leeds University, and Eve went into publishing. He worked initially as a rep in the West Country for Michael Joseph and then carried the list in central London. It was a natural step for Eve to start his own list.

The year of 1956 was a momentous one for him. The Merlin Press began publishing in the spring; in September his political world was rocked by the Soviet Union's invasion of Hungary. A large group of dissenters, including Eve, left the Communist Party and joined the loose association known as the 'New Left'. Thompson eloquently expressed the new movement's open-minded views and its support for democratic socialism.

Eve published a series of books from the New Left in the late Fifties and early Sixties, most notably the work of Georg Lukács, the Hungarian critic and philosopher, and *Socialist Register*, edited by Ralph Miliband and John Saville – 'a survey of movements and ideas'. *The Register* was first published in 1964; it became a key forum for the Left, and has published continuously since.

Eve was a man of broad interests and entrepreneurial flair. In the 1960s he teamed up with the BBC producer Hugh Burnett to publish the

Monk cartoon books that made a substantial contribution to Merlin's turnover at the end of each year. Eve published numerous books on English history, initiating a distinguished historical reprint series; and he also secured the English rights to much of Stendhal's work. This is to say nothing of the sailing imprint 'Seafarer Books' that latterly became a major part of Merlin's publishing activities.

Brought up on the rivers of England's east coast (his father, a proficient yachtsman, had retired to Orford in Suffolk, to run the Butley Oysterage), Eve had inherited a love of the sea and sailing. In his own inimitable way he combined all these elements in his work, and would regularly take landlubbing booksellers, publishers and political enthusiasts for a weekend's sailing on his beloved *Privateer*. He sailed across to Copenhagen and Amsterdam on visits to booksellers. Eve wrote a charming account of his and his family's adventures with *Privateer* in *An Old Gaffer's Tale* (1984), his own contribution to the Seafarer list.

In the mid-seventies, typically canny and in advance of the Yuppie invasion, Eve secured the freehold of a building on the Isle of Dogs where he published and warehoused the books, and took on distribution of other lists, notably Monthly Review Press and the distinguished American reprint list August M. Kelley. These were successful times for Merlin. Edward Thompson was in a prolific phase of writing and campaigning. Eve reissued in 1977 his marvellous biography of William Morris and published a series of his polemical essays - *The Poverty of Theory* (1978), *Writing by Candlelight* (1980) and *Zero Option* (1982).

The spread of a new political culture in the late Sixties had led to a proliferation of radical publishers and booksellers. Merlin was joined by NLB/Verso, Pluto, Writers and Readers, Journeyman Press etc. - lists whose titles sold well in campus bookshops and in the growing number of independent radical bookshops. Eve was a member of a different generation to those he perhaps regarded as the tyros of '68 but he was always willing to offer advice and guidance, and through the Merlin Press provided a bridge into much mainstream publishing of the time.

Eve's engaging manner and quick mind made him a successful salesman (I was always amazed at the orders he could bring back from a bookshop), a fine publisher and a great companion. He also had a fierce determination, which sustained him through all the political, publishing and business challenges he faced - and latterly in the face of severe illness and disability. Following the diagnosis of cancer in 1986 he showed quite extraordinary will power and courage in facing his growing incapacity, undergoing a series of treatments, and yet continuing to run his publishing business, and surviving withdrawal from an unsuccessful partnership with another publisher. Through all this he was unstintingly supported by his wife Pat.

He published for over 40 years and has left his mark through the Merlin Press. He began when publishing houses and firms embodied their owners' enthusiasms and when imprints had clear eponymous identities - a different world from today when lists are bought and sold as branding shells for some new corporate initiative. He was working right up to his death, preparing the new *Socialist Register* for the printer, and taking steps to ensure the Press's continuity.

David Musson
Colleague for ten years at Merlin Press
* * *

BOOKSELLER					13 NOVEMBER 1998

Martin Eve of the Merlin Press died on 29th October. After war service in the Navy, Martin worked initially as a rep for Michael Joseph. He started the Merlin Press in 1956, and published continuously until his death.

The core of the Merlin list was works of politics, history and philosophy associated with the New Left.

Merlin authors included Martin's lifelong friend E P Thompson, Georg Lukács, Ernest Mandel, István Mészáros, Sheila Rowbotham and Hilary Wainwright.

Always pragmatic and entrepreneurial, he supported his political publishing with a range of successful ventures including several translations of Stendhal; the famous 'Monk' cartoon books by BBC producer Hugh Burnett; and an excellent list in English history. He also developed the Seafarer imprint, which included numerous sailing narratives, including his own, *An Old Gaffer's Tale*.

Martin was a much respected figure in the world of independent and radical publishing, and the book trade. Despite the enervating effects of serious illness during the last decade, he continued publishing with the same enthusiasm, charm and strength of will that sustained the Merlin Press over 40 years.

David Musson
Who worked with Martin from 1975-1984
* * *

EAST ANGLIAN DAILY TIMES 30 OCTOBER 1998

A pensioner who inspired many people in Suffolk with his battle against cancer has died.

Martin Eve, 74, worked tirelessly at his publishing business in Rendlesham, near Woodbridge, and refused to be beaten by the cancer which steadily became worse.

He suffered from peripheral neuropathy for many years, which primarily affected movement in his hands and legs, and he had to rely upon crutches for 10 years until a few months ago.

Mr. Eve took proper exercise for the first time when he had a bicycle specially modified to allow him to pedal from a lying down position.

The recumbent 6ft long bicycle gave Mr. Eve, of Redwald Road, Rendlesham Park, independence. But then he had a fall in August and was confined to a wheelchair.

His widow Patricia Eve said yesterday: 'He was an inspiration to all of us, but he became so disabled that after his fall, he used to suck drinks through a straw - but Martin never complained.

'He kept working until the end. He was a truly remarkable man who had a happy and fulfilled life and did all the things he wanted to.'

Mr. Eve was brought up in Orford and as a child cycled 90 miles for a piano lesson in London, cycling back the next day.

He joined the Royal Navy, where he took part in the Algiers landing in November 1942 and the Second Front, D-Day landings. His membership of the Communist Party effectively barred him from any teaching job after the war and he set up his own publishing house in 1956. He had been a travelling rep for Michael Joseph publishers.

Mrs. Eve said: 'With hardly any financing behind it, Merlin made a slow start and each book essentially had to pay for the next.'

Mr. Eve became associated with the New Left and then the Peace Movement. Thirty years ago, he started up Seafarer Books which published narrative books on sailing.

Richard Smith
Chief reporter East Anglian

* * *

GAFFERS LOG   GEORGE JAGO

The last chapter of this Old Gaffer's tale has, I am sad to say, been written. Martin, who was diagnosed with lymphoma in 1986, kept smiling, sailing and working right until the end, when he died on 26 October. He owned *Privateer*, a converted Boston smack, which he kept at Tollesbury, Essex, and in 1984 wrote and published *An Old Gaffer's Tale*, in which he chronicled the pleasure that he and his family had derived from owning her. Born in London, Martin started his sailing on the River Alde in Suffolk, where his father, himself a notable yachtsman, retired to oversee the Butley Oysterage (see letter following).

He followed his mother's strong Socialist beliefs, which were of a very practical nature, all his life. Early in World War II, he falsified his age to join the Royal Navy and later, commissioned as an RNVR officer, he was at the D-Day landings. Demobilised in 1946, he then read history at Cambridge. In 1956 he set up his own publishing company, Merlin Press. Later an imprint Seafarer Books, was formed, which met the needs of his love of sailing, attracting many well-known maritime writers.

A man of strong principles and sincere and unstinting support to anyone in need, Martin will be sorely missed on the East Coast.

The Old Gaffers Association extend their sincere condolences to his wife Pat and his family.

Editor

LETTER FROM MARTIN
Seafarer Books, 2 Rendlesham Mews, Rendlesham.
Nr. Woodbridge, Suffolk IP12 2SZ
8 September 1998

Dear Brenda & George,

Good to see you yesterday. This is my contribution to the article on the *Sheena*. I was going to write to tell you that I have a very clear recollection of *Sheena* as a Bermudan boat in 1931. She had the next mooring to us at Orford and of course we were on friendly terms, even though she was Bermudan rigged. At the age of seven I naturally shared my father's prejudices and he had done almost all his cruising and racing before there was, as we called it, a Marconi rigged boat to be seen anywhere. She was then sailed by Robin Ross-Taylor but I suppose owned by his father Walter. She would have been Bermudan all the time she was at Orford in their ownership. I recall Robin standing on her truck, a feat I have never seen anywhere else. Since talking to you yesterday, I am pleased to hear that my long term memory was not mistaken.

Yours etc.
Martin

On this same day, Martin remarked to us how pleased he was that *Privateer* had found a good home.

Editor

* * *

EAST COAST OLD GAFFER'S ASSOCIATION

It is with great sadness that we have to report the death of Martin Eve. He typified much of what we like to think the OGA is about, with his adventures in the Boston smack yacht *Privateer*. For many years he sailed her out of Tollesbury, her annual cruises taking her to the continent and the West Country. However he and Pat were very much Eastcoasters of the finest sort, and *Privateer* could be seen in almost every creek and river on the East Coast on weekends throughout the year. Despite suffering crippling illness in his later years, he kept on sailing almost to the end, a great inspiration to all. He was always a great pleasure to talk to, his knowledge on traditional boats and the people who sailed them fascinating.

We quote from 'A Thought for Martin'

Martin died peacefully, surrounded by his family on 26 October 1998.

He approached his death with the same courage and determination with which he had coped with his illness and disabilities over the past twelve years.

He felt he had had a very happy and fulfilled life doing the best for the causes that were most important to him.

He continued working right up to his death, completing and sending two books to the printers.

Old Gaffers Association

* * *

POETRY FAREWELL

As a publisher Martin traded in words, but for him words were not commodities to be stored behind publishing house doors until they were sold. His feeling for their meaning, their rightness and their sound was his companion everywhere in his own writing and in his appreciation of the writing of others.

His prose flows as smoothly as a summer tide in his book about his beloved *Privateer*. His rare poetry was not the result of a sudden rush of fancy, but was a seed of thought planted, tended and pruned until it was exactly right in shape and fruit.

In his life Martin faced death more than many of us, first in a serious illness in boyhood; next in the unpredictability of naval action; lastly in the crises of twelve years of crippling illness. This experience was the seed of poems.

* * *

To Death

I met you long ago and looked you in the face;
Your eyes were empty, not cruel, not kind, just empty.
You passed me by but I knew you'd be back
When Mother Nature tells you to call me into rest.

* * *

Time

Passes
Will not wait
Can be saved or spent
Is the enemy
Takes its revenge;
Time is also
The river which heals all wounds.

* * *

Martin's awareness of the significance of the poet's voice in society is expressed in his own poem.

Diapason

You know the rocks and shallows
You warn
You show the narrow channel
The safe harbour
Sound out in the mist,
Make your voice heard

Raise your voice, poet,
Your warning sound
This is no clear day
When you can sleep.

Writers of poems which struck a chord in Martin's heart include two linked by service in the Special Operations Executive in the Second World War. At the London headquarters Leo Marks, a brilliant cryptographer, created the codes for communication with S.O.E. officers and wireless operators working dangerously in enemy-occupied countries. Frank Thompson, scholar and poet, was an S.O.E. officer. At the age of 23 he was captured while leading a mission in Bulgaria and was executed by firing squad.

One of the last books which Martin published is *Beyond The Frontier*, the story of Thompson's fatal mission, compiled from lectures given by Frank's brother, the late Edward Thompson, and edited by Edward's widow Dorothy, with some help from Martin. The book opens with this poem by Frank:

As one, who, gazing at a vista
Of beauty, sees the clouds close in
And turns his back in sorrow, hearing
The Thunderclaps begin

So we, whose life was all before us,
Our hearts with sunlight filled,
Left in the hills our books and flowers,
Descended, and were killed.

Write on the stone no words of sadness,
- Only the gladness due
That we, who asked the most of living,
Knew how to give it too.

Those who have read *Between Silk And Cyanide*, the book in which
Leo Marks describes his war years at S.O.E. headquarters, know that after
receiving news of the death in an air crash of the girl he loved dearly he
expressed his feelings in the following poem. Years later it became a
bond of feeling shared by Martin and Pat.

The life that I have
Is all that I have
And the life that I have
Is yours

The love that I have
Of the life that I have
Is yours and yours
and yours

A sleep I shall have
A rest I shall have
Yet death will be but
A pause

For the peace of my years
In the long green grass
Will be yours and yours
and yours.

The words of another war poet accompanied Martin on his return late in life to the land he had loved all his life, the wind-swept, sea-fashioned Suffolk shore 'from Orfordness to Shingle Street,' and its forested hinterland. He had known Shingle Street since boyhood, sailing there from Orford with his father. Its bare strangeness, its loneliness, its shifting shingle banks fascinated him. His father's ashes were scattered there. After Martin's return to Suffolk he went there whenever he could. His own ashes, too, will find a resting place there.

In 1941 Alun Lewis, the poet, knew this strip of coast as a soldier, a soldier who was to die in far-off Arakan Later in the war. He has left this haunting word picture of the shore which Martin knew so well.

Dawn on the East Coast

From Orford Ness to Shingle Street
The grey disturbance spreads uneasily
Washing the icy seas on Deben Head.

Cock pheasants scratch the frozen fields,
Gulls lift horny legs and step
Fastidiously among the rusted mines.

The soldier leaning on the sandbagged wall
Hears in the combers' curling rush and crash
His single self-centred monotonous wish;

And Time is a froth of such transparency,
His drowning eyes see what they wish to see,
A girl laying his table with a white cloth.

The light assails him from a flank,
Two carbons touching in his brain
Crumple the cellophane lanterns of his dream.

And then the day, grown feminine and kind,
Stoops with the gulfing motion of the tide
And pours his ashes in a tiny urn.

From Orford Ness to Shingle Street
The grey disturbance lifts its head
And one by one, reluctantly,
The living come back slowly from the dead.

A little more than half a century later it was Martin's turn to leave, but in peace, this land of shingle shore, of sea-shifted banks and sea-bitten cliff, of marsh and heath, of Saxon grave, of winding river, of forest and farm - a land where his ashes and his spirit stay.

It was the time of the carting of the beet.
The gale was strong from the south-west,
And breakers reared against the Sandling shore.
Leaves chased the clouds.
The reeds writhed in their beds
And in the boatyards
Rigging sang the song which Martin knew.
And he had sailed safely to his haven.

Walter Kemsley
Brother-in-law

1999 NEW BOOKS FROM MERLIN PRESS:

Chartist Legacy, the	Ashton, Fyson, Roberts	085036 484 1	12.95
Images of Chartism	Roberts, Thompson	085036 475 2	12.95
Socialist Register 1999	Panitch, Leys (ed)	085036 480 9	12.95

MERLIN PRESS BACKLIST:

A New Kind of Doctor	Tudor Hart	085036 300 4	9.95
Anti-Bolshevik Communism	Mattick	085036 223 7	9.95
Antonio Gramsci	Davidson	085036 215 6	9.95
Art & Society	Vazquez	085036 219 9	8.95
Atomic Crossroads	Valentine	085036 337 3	6.95
Background to Contemporary Greece Vol 1	Sarafis	085036 393 4	9.95
Background to Contemporary Greece Vol 2	Sarafis	085036 394 2	9.95
Behind the Lines	Bush	085036 306 3	9.95
Beyond Capital	Meszaros	085036 432 9	14.95
Beyond the Fragments	Rowbotham	085036 254 7	8.95
Beyond the Frontier	Thompson, E.P.	085036 461 2	8.95
Bram Fischer: A Life for Africa	Mitchison	085036 356 X	9.95
Bristol Oversea Trade (cl)	Carus-Wilson	085036 045 5	15.00
British Intervention in Greece(cl)	Richter	085036 301 2	25.00
Can Britain Feed Itself	Mellanby	085036 193 1	2.95
Customs in Common (cl)	Thompson, E.P.	085036 411 6	25.00
Democratic Review	Chartist Reprints	085036 098 6	20.00
Destruction of Reason (cl)	Lukács	085036 247 4	22.50
East Timor's Unfinished Struggle	Pinto	085036 479 5	9.95
Economic Crisis and Crisis Theory	Mattick	085036 269 5	8.95
Economics, Politics and Inflation	Mattick	085036 259 8	5.95
Enemy Within	Beckett	085036 477 9	9.95
Engineers at War	Croucher	085036 271 7	9.95
English Antique Furniture	Dean	085036 202 X	1.95
English Popular Art (cl)	Marx	085036 372 1	20.00
Erotocritos	Kornaros	085036 335 7	16.00
Essays on Thomas Mann	Lukács	085036 238 5	7.95
Folksong Plainsong	Chambers	085036 195 8	8.95
From History to Sociology	Antoni	085036 100 1	9.95
Goethe and his Age	Lukács	085036 071 4	8.95
History & Class Consciousness	Lukács	085036 197 4	9.95
Hobby Horse (cl)	Alford	085036 160 5	15.00

Title	Author	ISBN	Price
Homeworkers Worldwide	Rowbotham	085036 434 5	5.95
Human Guinea Pigs	Mellanby	085036 173 3	9.50
Images of Chartism	Roberts& Thompson	085036 475 2	12.95
Imperialism and the World Economy	Bukharin	085036 210 5	6.95
Joseph Ashby of Tysoe	Ashby	085036 180 X	9.95
Karl Marx & the Close of his system	Bohm-Bawerk	085036 206 7	9.95
Lancelot Hogben: Scientific Humanist	Hogben	085036 470 1	14.95
Lawfinders and Lawmakers (cl)	Cam	085036 041 2	15.00
Leninism under Lenin	Liebmann	085036 261 X	9.95
Liberties and Communities (cl)	Cam	085036 042 0	15.00
Loom of Language	Bodmer	085036 350 0	12.95
Manorial Studies (cl)	Levett	085036 063 3	15.00
Marx and Keynes	Mattick	085036 230 X	9.95
Marxist Economic Theory	Mandel	085036 166 4	11.95
Marx's Theory of Alienation	Meszaros	085036 191 5	9.95
Mathematics for the Million	Hogben	085036 380 2	12.95
Neo-Colonial Identity	Constantino	085036 221 0	8.95
Notes to the People (2 vols)	Chartist Reprints	085036 097 8	25.00
Ontology - Hegel	Lukács	085036 226 1	5.95
Ontology - Marx	Lukács	085036 227 X	5.95
Persons and Polemics	Thompson, E.P.	085036 439 6	12.95
Philosophy of Praxis	Vazquez	085036 216 4	9.95
Poverty of Theory (new edn)	Thompson, E.P.	085036 446 9	8.95
Prolegomena	Harrison	085036 263 6	12.95
Protest & Survival - Festschrift for E.P.T	Thompson, E.P.	085036 445 0	9.95
Red Republican & Friend of the People (2 vols)	Chartist Reprints	085036 096 X	25.00
Reviews and Articles	Lukács	085036 281 4	4.95
Revolution & Counter Revolution in Portugal	Kayman	085036 341 1	18.50
Samizdat Register I	Medvedev	085036 208 3	6.95
Science & Retreat From Reason	Gillot & Kumar	085036 433 7	10.95
Short History of Lit. Criticism	Hall	085036 056 0	6.95
Small Landowner (cl)	Johnson	085036 060 9	9.00
Socialist Register 1995	Panitch (ed)	085036 448 5	12.95
Socialist Register 1996	Panitch (ed)	085036 456 6	12.95
Socialist Register 1997	Panitch (ed)	085036 466 3	12.95
Socialist Register 1998	Panitch (ed)	085036 473 6	12.95
Solzhenitsyn (cl)	Lukács	085036 143 5	7.50
St Catherine's Monastery (cl)	Paliouras	085036 256 X	20.00
Stephen Langton (cl)	Powicke	085036 085 4	12.50
Studies in European Realism	Lukács	085036 211 3	8.95
The Chamberlain-Hitler Collusion	Finkel & Leibovitz	085036 468 X	12.95
The Death of Uncle Joe	Macleod	085036 467 1	9.95

The English Yeoman	Campbell	085036 289 X	9.95
The Heavy Dancers	Thompson, E.P.	085036 329 2	7.95
The Historical Novel	Lukács	085036 378 0	9.95
The Ideas of Victor Serge	Weissman (ed)	085036 483 3	12.00
The Meaning of Contemporary Realism	Lukács	085036 250 4	6.95
The Non-Jewish Jew	Deutscher	085036 274 1	7.95
The Oil Crisis (cl)	Bina	085036 323 3	18.50
The Romantics	Thompson, E.P.	085036 474 4	12.95
The Threshers Labour (cl)	Duck	085036 375 6	4.95
The Young Hegel	Lukács	085036 198 2	12.95
Themis	Harrison	085036 229 6	12.95
Theory and Practice Italian Communism	Davidson	085036 265 2	9.95
Theory of the Novel	Lukács	085036 236 9	7.95
Totemism	Levi-Strauss	085036 382 9	7.95
Understanding the French Revolution	Soboul	085036 381 0	9.95
Whistler at the Plough (cl)	Somerville	085036 304 5	35.00
William Morris	Thompson, E.P.	085036 205 9	12.95
Working Class of India	Sen	817074 189 0	12.95
Working in Metal(cl)	McGuffie	085036 312 8	17.50
Writer & Critic	Lukács	085036 237 7	8.95
Writing by Candlelight	Thompson, E.P.	085036 260 1	8.95
Zero Option	Thompson, E.P.	085036 288 1	7.95

Pamphlet

The Communist Manifesto	Marx & Engels	085036 478 7	1.00

Fiction

Broad and Alien is the World	Alegria	085036 282 2	9.95
Englishmen with Swords	Slater	085036 402 7	4.99
Sandwichman	Brierly	085036 391 8	6.99
Wild Goose Chase	Warner	085036 388 8	6.99
Winter Solstice	Cowlin	085036 408 6	5.99

1999 NEW BOOKS FROM SEAFARER BOOKS:

Celtic Ring (Hbk)	Larsson	085036437X	12.95
Marine Salvage (Hbk)	Reid	0924486996	14.95
Rescue And Recovery (Pbk)	Mulville	0850364620	8.95
Riddle of the Sands (Hbk)	Childers	0850364760	9.95
Søren Larsen (Pbk)	Cottier	0850364825	10.95
Topsail And Battleaxe (Pbk)	Cunliffe	0850364604	10.95
Travellers on a Trade Wind (Pbk)	Pirie	085036471X	10.95

SEAFARER BOOKS BACKLIST:

A Winter Away From Home	Unwin	0850364426	10.95
Build Your Own Boat	Nicolson	0850364582	9.95
Captain's Guide Liferafts	Cargal	0850364183	14.95
Coast Of Summer (Hbk)	Bailey	0850364507	12.95
The Compleat Cruiser	Herreshof	0850364221	8.95
Cruise Of The Snark	London	085036311X	9.95
Dear Dolphin	Mulville	0850364647	8.95
Discovery In The North Atlantic	Sharp	0921054890	7.95
Following The Sea	Doane	0920852904	9.95
Last of The Sailormen	Roberts	085036342X	5.95
Letters From High Latitudes	Dufferin	085036387X	7.95
Cruising Guide To The Caribbean	Stone	0924486570	25.00
I Remember The Tall Ships	Brookesmith	0850363276	8.95
Mate Of The Caprice	Brown	0850364442	6.95
North Star To Southern Cross	Mulville	0850364639	8.95
Northwest Passage Solo (Hbk)	Cowper	0850364299	14.95
Oak Island	Crooker	155109049X	7.95
Old Gaffer's Tale	Eve	0850364248	8.95
Prince Henry Sinclair	Pohl	1551091224	8.95
Return To Murmansk	Swain	0850364531	9.95
Sable Island Shipwrecks	Campbell	1551090961	8.95
Sailing Alone Around The World (Hbk)	Slocum	0911378200	9.95
Sailing Past	Waite	0850364280	4.95
Schooner Bluenose II	Jenson	1551090635	12.95
Schooner Integrity	Mulville	0850364256	8.95
Seascapes And Sailing Ships	Macaskill	0920852785	15.95
Single Handed Sailing	Mulville	0850364108	7.95
Slope Of The Wind	Seligman	0850364434	10.95
Small Wooden Boats	Walker	0921054548	14.95
Sutton Hoo	Green	0850362415	7.95
The Sailing Mystique	Robinson	0924486635	9.95
The Sailor's Weather Guide (Pbk)	Markell	0924486910	11.95
The Solitary Slocum	Blondin	1551090260	8.95
Thousand Dollar Yacht	Bailey	0850364590	8.95
Voyage Of The Cap Pilar	Seligman	0850364388	10.95